Great Thoughts and Reflections - Self Enquiry For All

The quest that includes ethics, adoration, meditation and mindfulness

Dr. Murali Krishnamurthy and N. Nandakumar

Table of Contents

Foreword by Acharya Vasuda Chaitanya, Founder,
    Viva Vedanta Foundation 5

Preface – Authors' Notes 7

Note to the Reader from the Authors 11

World, Work and Service 13

Meditation/Goal 43

Adoration/Love 82

Mindfulness/Witness 124

Self-Enquiry/Know Yourself 152

Foreword by Acharya Vasuda Chaitanya, Founder, Viva Vedanta Foundation

Dr Murali Krishnamurthy, as I have always known him, has been personable, focused, and hardworking. He embodies the image of a sincere teacher, a mentor to his students, with utter humility, and most importantly, genuineness.

"Great Thoughts and Reflections" as the very name suggests is a compilation of wise sayings or wisdom quotes, carefully picked by the authors, Murali and Shri N. Nandakumar. Quotes from famous people, authors, and influential figures, whom we could all learn something from. They encourage readers to take the journey with this inspired book, just as they did. In the very reading of this book, the enquiry into the Self shall begin.

Quotations often offer a second voice that echoes our thoughts, beliefs, and views. They provide a better way of saying things. They give us concise and suitable phrasing. The wise words chosen in the book may help us gain perspective from people who see things differently and help us make better choices

We can use these quotes and their understanding, to impart knowledge, reinforce values for ourselves, use them in debates and discussions, or console or inspire others.

This book, a result of immense efforts and time, speaks of the generous and benevolent nature of the authors. Without an intention to do good, it is difficult to make a ready reckoner of wisdom quotes. Intention to inspire and motivate, with no expectations of a reward, other than just that the book be read and made use of. Hence, I urge you all to read this book. For pleasure, for inspiration, for guidance, for mental recreation whatever that reason may be. You may just find it all here.

Preface – Authors' Notes

Dr. Murali Krishnamurthy:

It is a great joy that I feel today. A simple idea of sharing some good thoughts and quotes along with good morning wishes through WhatsApp – before smartphone days it used to be emails - which I started about a decade back, has crystallized into a book now.

If I missed even a day, I used to get queries, 'Why there is no message today? Are you ok?', etc. This encouraged me to read and get the best quotes and thoughts to share.

Nandu (Nandakumar the co-author of this book) and I go back almost four decades. We joined the banking industry together in the mid-80s.

He started expanding on the quotes with beautiful, deep, and relevant spiritual and philosophical explanations to these daily. In our WhatsApp group, our ex-colleague and dear friend Ramakrishnan suggested one day, 'Why don't you bring these out in a book?'. And so began this journey.

We selected 108 quotes from the ones that I had shared in the past five years and Nandu literally rewrote his commentary. And further to that I added my own thoughts and understanding from what little I had learned and comprehended. We have kept the format as it is, without merging our commentaries.

We leave it to the reader to read, understand, and internalize in his/her own way. I am extremely grateful to Acharya Vasuda Chaitanya, founder, of Viva Vedanta Foundation, under whose feet, I had the privilege to learn The Holy Bhagavad Gita and who has inspired and guided me through the past decade.

Nandu and I are indebted to Sri. Ravi Prabhu for his painstaking work in correcting our English and proofreading the book, to ensure it is error-free.

I also acknowledge gratefully the support and encouragement from my wife Vijayalakshmi and my children Vandana Murali and Raghav Murali who have stood by me like a rock, throughout.

N Nandakumar:

In the course of my practice of self-enquiry, I realised that all the ethical and spiritual practices I had followed, involved one common factor - turning inward. My journey in life had slipped to such abysmal levels that my consciousness was ready to say anything to tide over the moment. By the time I met and benefited from my friend, VKLV Kumar, I had touched spiritual rock bottom. It is the recovery from the abyss that allowed me to see the same energy in all ethical and spiritual practices.

It is this turning inward that emboldened me to connect any quote of upliftment posted by my friend Dr. Murali Krishnamurthy in the group, to the Self of all. For instance, when I started the practice of speaking what was true to me and acting ethically in the company of VKLV Kumar, I had to let go of the world and God and see what 'I' was speaking or doing. My journey to the reality underlying the world and the reality of God had begun when I turned inward towards my self.

The reader would stand to benefit by relying on one's inner light to ponder over these enquiries. Form or confirm your own inner rules. Live those rules in the world. Keep enquiring whether there is one rule or energy available which tradition calls as God. If you see any worth in directly starting the quest 'Who am I?', start it by all means. My life journey was clarified by this direct path. Of course, one could enjoy reading through the thoughts of the great ones just for the sheer joy of it. Thousands of years of spiritual guidance lie open before us in just a few pages.

I am grateful for what our life is. It is an opportunity to learn and come upon the Truth. The application of Self Enquiry to day-to-day living started with my association with Dr. Sarada Natarajan and the Ramana Maharshi Centre for Learning. From the year 2007, the opportunity to serve Ramana Maharshi Centre for Learning has allowed me to be at that spot where the rubber meets the road; where the spiritual teachings have their confluence and absorption of every moment of our day-to-day life. It is from my interactions with the team of Self Enquiry practitioners like Dr. Sarada Natarajan, Dilip

Simha, Venkatesh Deshpande, Kameshwar, Dr. Ambika Kameshwar, Dr. Poorna, and many keen aspirants that I have tried to connect these great inspirational quotes through Ethics, Adoration, Meditation, and Mindfulness to Self Enquiry, which, in my experience, includes all.

Note to the Reader from the Authors

How to read meditatively, mindfully, and self-attentively

We have expressed our points of view on the uplifting quotes. Each one of you can have your own version. There are over seven billion possible versions. There are indeed infinite versions say Galileo and Chomsky. If you feel like it, write your own version and read it. You can plunge ahead with these two versions as pointers to those infinite versions. Murali has taken up the task of looking at the quotes through spiritual teachings and faith., whereas Nandu has relied on his writing from that important angle and placed his views before the reader.

Each of the 108 passages of the book begins with quotes on the upliftment of the life of the reader. The quotes are explained through ethics, philosophy, psychology, meditation, mindfulness, and self-enquiry. The reader would often come upon areas of 'not-knowing'. How to read through the understandable and not understandable areas? Of course, as you read these passages again and again, the meaning will become clearer till the whole book is an open secret.

1. When you are reading with the love of reading, you are happily meditating with the support of word forms.
2. You will run into places of 'not knowing' or 'not understanding'. Hold that 'not knowing' without expecting an answer and you are practising meditation without the support of word form.
3. When you read the description of the quotes without judgement as 'good' or 'bad' keeping the mind in the present, you are practising mindfulness-reading.
4. When you reach portions that you hit with 'not knowing', be without judging the 'not knowing' as good or bad in the present. That is mindfulness of the void.

5. The reader is always present in the act of reading. If you read without leaving the inner quest of 'Who is reading?', that is reading with self-attention.

6. When you hit the place of 'not knowing' and remain self-attentive, that is realising that the Self remains even when no objects of attention exist. When this is effortless, that is Self-realisation. Here, the reading goes on effortlessly in areas of knowing and not knowing, as the real Self illumines everything - knowledge and ignorance.

7. Reading is a slice of living. While reading meditatively, mindfully, and self-attentively, put it to practice in day-to-day living by living meditatively, mindfully, and self-attentively. The Self is ever real. Read and live your way to the Real Self.

World, Work and Service

1. *Nobody can do everything, but everybody can do something......*
NNK: These words of hope are from Max Lucado an American Author and Minister at Oak Hills Church in San Antonio, Texas.

To the parent of an autistic child, the problem appears not only gargantuan but unsolvable, as human knowledge - all sciences and psychology put together - does not have a definite solution to this problem. The child seems underdeveloped in sensory faculties but, generally speaking, more developed in emotions and skills like music. The child picks up and reacts to the stress or happiness in the parents but seems to have compulsive actions in the sensory body which prevents learning.

Therapists, psychologists, and researchers are still grappling with the problem. What began as a small percentage of intellectual parents giving birth to autistic children, has been spreading with more and more parents being intellectual and more children being born in the autistic spectrum.

Parents cannot solve the problem completely. However, by keeping a clear mind and not expecting the child to become something, the parent can be with the child in a moment of peace. The child can receive this presence that is unconditional love. The parent could slip into anxiety and see the child picking it up. Once again, the parent can get the mind back to not expecting anything of the child, but give unconditional presence.

Whenever an anxiety arises, enquire, 'For whom is this anxiety? Who am I? Whenever the mind asks as to when this ordeal for the child is going to get over, enquire for whom is this worry. Who am I? Self-attention is the unconditional love in which the child can flower. A single thought stilled for a moment by enquiry takes one a long way towards natural self-attention which is unconditional love. One may not realise the Self in one go. But, surely, one can quell one thought in self-enquiry…

Dr. MK: This is a particularly powerful thought. We normally do not observe many things during our day-to-day lives but simply look through them…. not really giving any thought about what we see/look at. But there are fabled instances where one small act done by someone has changed the lives of ordinary people. Dr. APJ Abdul Kalam, lovingly remembers his teacher who helped him to pay fees and study. That enabled him, later to become a top scientist and the President of our country.

Similarly, we see stories of Dr. Babasaheb Ambedkar, who was helped by his teacher so that he could succeed. He is known as the father of our Constitution. Umpteen anecdotes are there that indicate that if only we as common, normal people, instead of just "looking through" things but "looking at" things and taking action, many lives could be transformed.

2. ***"One who conquers his desires is braver than one who conquers his enemies because the hardest victory is over self."***

NNK: These words connecting inner victory and outer victory are from the ancient Greek philosopher and polymath, Aristotle.

We begin life by conquering enemies. If one considers the hurdles of life as enemies, then all of life is but victory over enemies. However, who are our enemies? How do we determine our enemies? Our desires, prejudices, judgements, and even impulses decide who or what is our enemy.

Our desires - when we bring all our inner thinking as this single manifestation - are limited but infinite. Desires are limited because they limit our selves and can only point to limited objects and objectives. Desires are Infinite, as they keep coming endlessly. Unless we are free of our desires, how do we know who our enemy is? Moreover, desire and its completion never bring contentment. Many a time, fulfilling desires like smoking is like pouring petrol over fire as it increases the dependence on the object.

To observe and let go of desires, one should catch desire at its root. When a thought arises, irrespective of what thought it is, let go of the thought by enquiring, 'For whom is this thought?'. It is always for me. Enquire, 'Who am I?'. Victory over desires is complete freedom from all thoughts including the root thought, the 'I' thought, and the ego. Such victory is true victory. To no one is the enemy outside. The true enemy is the root desire to have a separate form - the ego. Victory over that is true victory.

Dr. MK: Our scriptures keep talking about desires and how to overcome them. In The Bhagavad Gita in verse 62 of Chapter 2, Sri Krishna says,

dhyāyato vishayān pumsah sangas teshūpajāyate

sangāt sañjāyate kāmah kāmāt krodho 'bhijāyate

The meaning of this verse - While contemplating the objects of the senses, one develops an attachment to them. Attachment leads to desire, and from desire arises anger.

The Vedas consider anger, desire, greed, lust, etc. as *'maanas roga'* or diseases of the mind. Shree Krishna has given perfect and penetrating insight into the functioning of the mind. He explains that when we repeatedly contemplate that there is happiness in some object, the mind becomes attached to it. For example, if in a class of boys and girls, why only one boy should be attracted to a particular girl? He feels he is in love with her and can't live without her, whereas all the boys and girls interact in the class and no other boy has such a feeling towards that girl. The fact is that this boy repeatedly thought that there was happiness in the girl, and so his mind became attached to her. And the more the desire increases, it leads to other negative thoughts like jealousy, vengeance, anger, and revenge.

So, it is important for us to conquer ourselves and our desires. One who does that can conquer himself and his enemies.

3. *"Action not backed by knowledge and knowledge not translatable into action, both cannot stand the test of time.".*

NNK: This quote is taken from the words of Sri. Pandurang Sastri Athawale of the Swadhyaya movement. His teachings were primarily based on the Bhagavad Gita.

When my typing of this message is not backed by the required knowledge, the message will surely be worthless. This is easy to understand. That, knowledge that cannot be translated into action too, will not stand the test of time and may be difficult to understand.

In a panel discussion on the life and teachings of a famous teacher, one of the panelists was asked whether the teacher had lived by his teachings. The panelist opined as to where is the necessity. Is it not enough that the teachings were good? She was affirming that she believed that this teacher had not lived by his teachings but also thought it was alright! The entire audience was stunned into a painful silence. So, unless knowledge is translated as lived truth, such knowledge is useless tinsel. In fact, such ones who know but live the opposite are worse troublemakers than those who do not know. It is difficult to live by your knowledge. But, only by so living, is the individual transformed from animal to human and from human to divine.

Dr. MK: In The Bhagavad Gita chapter 4 verse 16 Sri Krishna says
kiṁ karma kim akarmeti kavayo 'pyatra mohitāḥ
tat te karma pravakṣhyāmi yaj jñātvā mokṣhyase 'śhubhāt
What is action and what is inaction? Even the wise are confused in determining this. Now I shall explain to you the secret of action, by knowing which, you may free yourself from material bondage.

And about knowledge, Sri Krishna says
na hi jñānena sadṛiśhaṁ pavitramiha vidyate
tatsvayaṁ yogasansiddhaḥ kālenātmani vindati
In this world, there is nothing as purifying as divine knowledge. One who has attained purity of mind through the prolonged practice of Yog, receives such knowledge within the heart, in due course of time.

Knowledge has the power to purify, elevate, liberate, and unite a person with God. It is thus supremely sublime and pure. However, a distinction needs to be made between two kinds of knowledge—theoretical information and practical realization.

There is one kind of knowledge that is acquired by reading the scriptures and hearing from the Guru. This theoretical information is insufficient by itself. It is just as if someone has memorized a cookbook but has never entered the kitchen. Such theoretical knowledge of cooking does not help in satiating one's hunger.

So, when we say that knowledge is without action and action not backed by knowledge, we must ask what is this knowledge? It is clear from The Gita that the knowledge that purifies you is divine knowledge and that is given by HIM. And without that knowledge, no action is useful. Any action taken without that is fruitless.

4. ***"The tragedy of human history is decreasing happiness amid increasing comforts."***

NNK: These words of wisdom are from Swamy Chinmayananda, a Hindu spiritual leader and teacher.

From the times of the Industrial Revolution and Intellectual Expansion, humans have sought and found more and more comforts in day-to-day life. Travel has changed from a necessity for survival to an opportunity for entertainment in great comfort. Vehicles have become fast and air-conditioned. Homes have been built to provide a haven of comfort and a special climate that stepping out into what is common to all has become a veritable hell. Instant foods and food delivered to the doorstep have added to comforts to no end. Sofas have become softer and the screens of Televisions occupy whole walls.

Physical comforts are not the only area of increase of comfort. Both men and women have become more and more egoistic, self-important, and selfish. The sense of sacrifice in relationships has receded to such lows that more than half of the marriages fail, with developing economies quickly catching up with the developed ones.

Man, wrongly feels that more choices mean more happiness. Psychologists find differently. Less choice, or no choice available, is happiness is their finding. Less self-importance and selfishness may mean less comfort and more sacrifice but it surely leads to happiness in long-lasting relationships. The only way is to spread wisdom about this unintelligent way of life that we are leading.

For whom is this seeking of comfort over happiness? Who am I? Take the ego to the source. One is not separate from the rest. One understands that one is part of the evolution of all of life. One leads a life of ever-present, choice-less acceptance, choice-free awareness as the undivided Self which is true happiness.

Dr. MK: It has become the nature of man to be always looking for something more. If he has a house, he wants a bigger one. If he has a car, he wants a bigger car. This constant yearning is what keeps him unhappy. If we ask ourselves, 'Do these materialistic things give me happiness?', the true answer is NO. Sri Ramana says 'The particular event-thing giving you happiness and well-being did not belong to an absolute reality but to a relative, contingent truth. Now do you want fleeting, discontinuous happiness that comes and goes, or do you want to be in constant bliss?'.

Modern technology has brought us so much to make life easier and more enjoyable, yet it would seem that, if anything, people are more dissatisfied than ever. Why is this? What is happiness? What makes us happy or unhappy?

Albert Schweizer suggested that "Happiness is nothing more than good health and a bad memory." Socrates that "Happiness is an unrepented pleasure."? (But then what is 'pleasure'?) William Lyon Phelps said "The happiest people are those who think the most interesting thoughts. Those who decide to use leisure as a means of mental development, who love good music, good books, good pictures, good company, good conversation, are the happiest people in the world."

5. ***"When deeds and words are in accord, the whole world is transformed."***

NNK: This is a quote from Zhuangzhi which contains teachings of Taoism.

The ego arises; from the ego, other thoughts arise, from thoughts, words are spoken, from words spoken, the world expects actions of accord. To others and the world, one's words and actions are the only perceptible part of the individual. If the individual speaks words and does not act in accord, the world of actions and the world of relationships is in discord or disorder.

Not only are things in order when actions are in accord with words but relationships too. Each relationship is built on trust. Trust is built by making and keeping promises over whole lifetimes. So, the physical, financial, social, and psychological worlds depend on actions that are in accord with words. Words arise from thoughts. Thoughts arise from the rising of the 'I' thought. If the ego is under the influence of impulses, how can actions be in accord with the words? One will say one thing but be compelled to do another. All impulses are observed and erased in self-enquiry. For whom is this thought? Who am I? Only when one is not a slave to one's impulses and inclinations can one act in accord with one's words.

Dr. MK: If we contemplate deeply, we will realise that many times, we do some things which are not in line with what we said. In India, we have this notorious habit of saying, '5 minutes' for everything. But do we really do those in 5 minutes? People may say it is only a reference point and not actually 5 minutes. But we know very well for a fact that we will NOT be able to do that in 5 minutes but STILL, we say, 5 minutes to give a false sense of comfort to the listener.

Can we at least be truthful in saying what we do and doing what we say?

6. ***"Be glad of life because it gives you the chance to love, to work, to play, and to look up at the stars."***

NNK: These words imbued with shades of optimism are from Henry J VanDyke who considers himself to be a meliorist. He describes meliorism in this way; 'I'm not an optimist, there's too much evil in the world and me. Nor am I a pessimist; there is too much good in the world and God. So, I am just a meliorist, believing that He wills to make the world better, and trying to do my bit to help and wishing that it were more.'

It becomes clear that, from such a perspective, though the individual and the world have evil within, there is also much good in the world and God that each one has to work for the improvement of the world by being glad for the opportunity to improve oneself and the world by love, work, play and always looking up to the stars. This way they improve themselves and the world surrenders to God, the Supreme Good.

'Evil' and 'good' arise as thoughts only after the 'I' thought arises. For whom is this thought? Who am I? This enquiry keeps taking one beyond thought, both good and evil, or about the concepts of 'world' or 'God'. One abides in that limitless consciousness-existence beyond good and bad. Such a one understands that only by repeatedly holding the good with the belief that God wants each one to improve himself and the world, one gets the strength of penance to go beyond the duality of both 'good' and 'evil'. Such a one naturally encourages the efforts of others to hold love, good work, and optimism in the belief that God wants improvement of the world and the individual through meliorism as followed by Henry Vandyke, William James, and others like them as a path to God.

Dr. MK: What is the purpose of your life or anyone's life? Why are you here? Even if you believe that you are born by chance, is there nothing else to it? This is one conundrum about our lives, for which there is no clear and satisfactory answer unless you have read and assimilated the wisdom of the Bhagavad Gita, or any Hindu, Buddhist, or Jain scripture, and understood why we are subject to karma and why we are advised to engage in sacrificial actions without any selfish motive or intention.

When you try to answer the question, you may manage to find an answer, but you may also find it difficult to get rid of the nagging feeling that it may not be the right or perfect answer. However thoughtful and well-intended it may be, the response invariably arises in the domain of the mind and ego rather than the soul. Therefore, it is subject to the limitations of your knowledge and awareness, and egoism, desire, and delusion.

If you want to find a genuine answer to this question, you must pay mindful attention to the world around you and to all things that exist here, and learn from your observation the interdependence and interrelatedness of the whole existence, which are at the crux of it. You are not alone here, and you cannot live alone. Everything in creation is directly or indirectly connected to the rest of creation, just like the spokes in a wheel. Your actions affect others, just as theirs affect you. Therefore, in every religion you will find a great emphasis on the importance of virtuous and responsible living. By nonviolence, we mean not hurting or disturbing others, and not being disturbed by them. It is possible only when you practice other related virtues such as compassion, truthfulness, etc.

It also leads to another important conclusion. Your purpose cannot be separate or disconnected from the rest of the world. If you want to find your true purpose, you must see your own life from a broader perspective of the whole world, and see yourself about it. You will find the true answer only when you include others in it and align yourself to the larger aims and interests of the world and all life on earth.

This is what all living beings are supposed to do, including humans. They are supposed to be a part of God's symphony, the Bhagavad Gita. However, we are a different species. We do not live by instinct alone, nor can we be bound to a particular Dharma against our will. That choice has to be made by each of us. We are also programmed to be distinct and separate and pursue our own goals and interests according to our knowledge, discretion, and desires.

We find a purpose or some purpose according to our desires and intentions to create our own life stories. In most cases, that purpose remains selfish, self-centered, or egotistical. It is primarily meant to fulfill our desires and serve our interests.

In choosing our purpose or finding it, we do not go beyond our egoistic thoughts and selfish desires, nor do we think of the larger aims of our existence. We remain constricted and narrow-minded, as we try to make the most out of our otherwise purposeless lives.

We are not separate from the world. Our actions create their own ripples. Everyone and everything counts in the continuity of life. Even science affirms it. However, we ignore that underlying connection, as we become caught in the wheels of life. From the microorganisms to the large mammals, millions of beings are born every day and millions die, leaving behind no history or memory of their own. Some of them cannot be even seen or known. Yet, every one of them performs a definitive role (dharma) in Nature and leaves their footprint. The world thus thrives upon the collective Dharma of all. When we all do our parts, we create harmony, peace, and happiness and make the world a fit place to live.

Millenniums ago, the seers and sages of India, who lived closer to Nature in the deep forests of the Gangetic plains and Himalayan foothills, realized this fundamental truth. They believed that the duty of every human being on earth was to serve the larger interests of the world by performing a set of functions or obligatory duties, rather than pursuing their own selfish goals. They considered it the Dharma (moral duty) of humans. That Dharma has to be in harmony with God's own Dharma so that it would lead to order and regularity, peace, and happiness for everyone.

Human beings are endowed with intelligence, with which they can discern their obligatory duties, which are essential for the order and regularity of the world. Their lives are not meant for the narrow pursuit of selfish desires. Instead, living in a world which they do not own and which they cannot claim as theirs, they are supposed to live their lives as a sacrifice in service to God, the true owner, for the greater good of all.

To that God, we must make our offerings through our duties and obligations. That God, we must selflessly serve with dedication and devotion, and without showing any deference or distinction of high or low. By performing our actions as an offering and sacrifice, we must serve all that He represents here and above.

As we live in harmony with all things, doing our part and upholding our Dharma in the larger interests of all existence, we become free from the evil of selfishness and from the suffering and the chaos that may arise from our indulgence in it. It is what we call *"nishkama karma,"* which means performing actions as a sacrifice without desiring their fruit. The Bhagavad Gita states that God (Isvara) himself follows this principle to set an example for others. He performs his actions with detachment and upholds the creation for the sake of all the beings that depend upon it.

The Bhagavad Gita thus conveys a very important lesson about the purpose of human life. It is meant to be lived in the larger interests of God's creation. We are not supposed to live solely for ourselves or our selfish aim. Since the same Self exists in all, we cannot ignore the underlying connection and the unity of life. We must ensure we live in harmony our with environment, without hurting and harming, without encroaching upon their space, without taking what does not belong to us, without deceiving and envying, and without becoming a burden or a problem to others.

Your life's purpose is not to live for yourself, but to be useful and helpful in the sacrifice of life, transcending selfishness, egoism, and desires, engaging in actions with choiceless awareness and feeling oneness with everything around you, as if you have stepped into the all-inclusive vision and consciousness of God. If you do not believe in God, you may substitute the word with Nature or the universe.

Therefore, if you want to find a purpose, find one which is larger than your own life, and which can help you achieve peace and happiness for yourself and others. Do not aim for your pleasure or happiness. Selfishness makes you small and builds walls of separation and delusion around you. It puts you in competition with others and pits you against forces that you cannot control.

You can do it in numerous ways, sometimes by letting them be, sometimes by teaching them wisdom, sometimes by saving them from problems, and sometimes by just sharing with them love and laughter. This is how we are supposed to live, to be a beautiful and melodious note or a sacred chant in the symphony of God.

7. ***"Politics without principles, education without character, science without humanity, and commerce without morality are not only useless but positively dangerous."***

NNK: These words on the power of service to Society are from Sri Sai Baba of Puttaparthi, a Guru from India whose organisation sees service as the path to spiritual growth.

Politics is a power. Education is a power. Commerce is a power. As the Buddhist teaching goes, each one of us is given a key to heaven. However, the same key opens the doors to hell too. The individual has powers like politics, education, and commerce with which he can serve society and uplift himself spiritually. If the powers are used for good, society benefits and the individual serving the universal family uplifts himself, feeling one with the rest. If the powers are used to injure others, society is injured and the individual goes down spiritually as he moves away from the truth of the universal family.

So, politics without principles, education that does not build character but merely gives information, and commerce without morality or honesty lead to the downfall of the individual and society.

Any power has to be used to open the gates of heaven, not hell. So far as the individual feels separated from the universe, this test of good and bad needs to be applied to each action. When the individual has not completely transcended his impulses, how will he ensure good use of powers as he himself is a slave to his impulses? Erase the individuality which falsely separates one from the rest. When one realises the one Self, all use of powers like politics, education, or commerce will automatically emanate with principles, character, and morality of being one with the rest of creation.

Dr. MK: Bhagavan Sri Sathya Sai Baba, talks about the principles that one has to imbibe in oneself. Swami Vivekananda also has enunciated similar thoughts. The full quote - "Education without character, politics without principles, commerce without morality, Science without humanity, religion without love, culture without unity, administration without justice, knowledge without applications, patriotism without sacrifice are not only useless but positively dangerous" says Sri Sathya Sai Baba.

Today's education in our country has produced more educated people without having an in-depth idea of education and mechanised humans without having traits of humanity. It appears that our country is passing through a phase of serious apolitical crisis called value crisis. Everywhere there is a shadow of the missing spirit of life as if the true aim of human beings is to make wealth effortlessly, swiftly without any hurdle, and enjoy a comfortable living standard without adhering to the very basic philosophy of life. Bharat, so-called India, is losing its cultural supremacy and spiritual diversity in the global arena. Deep earnestness and sincerity by stakeholders of education for one of our vital national problems in a new light is the need of the day.

8. *Where there is righteousness in the heart, there is beauty in the character. When there is beauty in the character, there is harmony in the home. When there is harmony in the home, there is order in the nation. When there is order in the nation, there is peace in the world."*

NNK: These powerful words on how to bring peace in the world are from Dr. A.P.J. Abdul Kalam, scientist and past President of India.

He points out that each individual must have righteousness at heart for the whole world to be at peace. If one looks at how everyone is going to be righteous at heart, the problem appears complicated. But, when each one realises that this great human being is addressing me and wants me to be righteous at heart, the solution is really simple. Each Cyanobacteria lived only for 15 days. Each one took in carbon dioxide and let out oxygen that it had generated with the energy of sunlight. Together, over a billion years they brought oxygen levels on earth appropriate for the existence of higher mammals and created the ozone layer which protected these 'higher' organisms from harmful solar radiation. Let me have righteousness at heart.

Let each breath and action from me arise from this righteousness and morality. My family becomes harmonious with people who strive to have a good character made of righteous deeds. Wherever these members go and with whomever they come in contact, they carry this righteousness, good character, and harmony. Such a wave of behaviour imbued with harmony brings order to the nation. Orderly nations act to build peace in the world.

We also learn from Carl Jung that all humans are connected in the collective subconscious. Each right thought gets recorded. Each leaves a journey in the subconscious which could be followed by other introspective humans. So, it is important and enough to be righteous at heart. But I see that my mind comes in the way of my being righteous. Many a time, it makes the effort to be righteous but often it fails. To abide in a righteous life, one should go beyond the mind and ego.

For whom is this thought? Who am I? This takes one to the subconscious where we are all one. As each thought arises from the subconscious, one should let the thought go by asking, 'For whom is this thought? Who am I?'. The subconscious is crossed by persistent self-enquiry. The undivided light of the Self, the unbroken peace, then reveals itself. Such a one is a source of peace to the outside world and those seeking righteousness, character, harmony, order, and peace through introspection of the collective subconscious and the Self beyond.

Dr. MK: The concept of oneness has been elaborately explained in our epics. Oneness shows us the meaning of connection, in every sense of the word.

In essence, oneness is a feeling of interconnectedness – a transcendence of boundaries or dividers. It is usually experienced as an intense heart-opening and awareness of the inherent goodness of all beings. We gain the ability to see beauty everywhere, in everything and everyone. In that state of mind, it is easy to imagine a pathway to end all human conflict. Not surprisingly, the feeling of oneness is the source of a vast array of spiritual and philosophical musings.

Being one with the world, with the environment, and with the *Brahmandam* at large is the key to the Hindu way of evolution. Creating harmony with everything leads us to become part of them and we evolve into ONE being without any difference. Bhagavad- Gita underscores that there is unity amongst all living beings as God resides in all. The essence of man's nature, or our core nature or ***SUBHAVA**,* is divine, which is the same in all. The difference between one man and the other is only due to our acquired nature or Samskaras which are different in each person. So, if we are united and see God in everything and everyone, there is no need to create harmony. It automatically happens as we have created oneness.

9. ***"The very centre of your heart is where life begins….the most beautiful place on earth.."***

NNK: These words are from the great Sufi poet Rumi.

I search for the source of life all around. I understand that the purpose of my birth must be to find that source or search for it to the best of my ability. To come to this point, that the purpose of my birth must be to find the source of life, I have roamed all around. I have sought money; I have sought success at all costs. I have roamed to many places of pilgrimage. I have read many books. I have tried to meet great mentors. I have sought beauty in places and objects. Finally, I understand that outside of me is the three-dimensional world. All higher dimensions of life have to be searched for inside me. Even a great mentor outside is understood only according to the maturity of my mind and heart.

With my mind, I measure. I analyse. I may get some preliminary data on life. But it is the heart with which I should practice or learn to live and love. I may analyse that speaking the truth and living ethically is good. But, unless I live it with all my heart, I can't find the source of life. When all measurements of the mind cease and there is no judgement, the heart is full of life.

All other thoughts, including time and place; including thoughts of others great and small, arise only after the 'I' thought arises from the heart. This heart is not a blood-pumping organ. It is unconditional love, it is undivided awareness, it is existence beyond birth and death. It is the most beautiful 'place'.

Dr. MK: The heart whispers, this way, the mind says, no way.

The heart affirms, this is right, the mind reasons, this is impossible.

The heart urges, please, the mind decides, I can't.

We all have a subconscious mental framework of who we can and can't be and then we operate from that framework, often limiting ourselves in ways we don't have to be limited. We automatically make assumptions and predictions about how our lives will be based on our past experiences, unless we interrupt this pattern through conscious choice.

We create our own versions of a realistic life based on what we have seen and been told to be true. We think that the way life is, is an objective reality, but it is actually deeply personal; it is subjective, and thus subject to change as we do.

That's where the heart comes in. Our hearts see opportunities our minds have written off because they don't guide us based on what has already happened but by what still can. Not by the past but by the realm of current possibilities.

We are capable of creating futures that are vastly different from our pasts, and we transcend the barriers we have placed on ourselves when we allow our hearts to inform our minds instead of the other way around. We transform our realities when we have the courage to listen to the intuitive inkling that tells us something's off even when our lives appear to be right on track according to the world.

10. ***The cosmos is within us. We are made of star stuff. We are a way for the universe to know itself."***

NNK: This great thought is by the Scientist Carl Sagan who strived to make science simple and available to the common man.

We can see in the first part of this quote that we are made of star-stuff and the cosmos inside us can be understood through his own words. 'The nitrogen in our DNA, the calcium in our teeth, the iron in our blood, the carbon in our apple pies were made in the interiors of collapsing stars. We are made of star stuff. Thus, inside us is all star-stuff.

Understanding oneself is understanding the cosmos. Carl Sagan and a few other scientists of his time agree that humans are a way for the cosmos to know itself. Thought energy does not seem to have its origin in the collapse and re-assembling of stars. From where do thoughts arise? All thoughts arise after the rise of the 'I' thought. For whom is this attachment through thought to the body or cosmos? For whom is this thought? Who am I? It is after the 'I' arises on waking up that the attachment to the body made of star stuff arises. The source of the 'I' is the source of everything. It is the consciousness-existence beyond the body made of star stuff and the mind made of other thoughts, both arising after the rise of the 'I' thought.

Dr. MK: In Chapter 10, verse 21 of the Bhagavad Gita, Sri Krishna says, 'Among the shining gods I am Vishnu; Of luminaries, I am the sun; Among the storm gods I am Marichi; And in the night sky I am the moon'.

From the earliest times, men and women must have wondered about the sun, the moon, and the stars in the heavens, the forces governing the storms, and the cycles of light and darkness. Even those of us who are not astronomically inclined must have had moments when we asked the sun, "What are you doing there?" or the stars, "Are you friendly with one another?" Now, in this century, astronomy has developed high-powered instruments for looking beyond the galaxy we live in to probe a universe much vaster and more wonderful than we had ever imagined—a universe in which there are billions of other galaxies, each with millions of solar systems, all held together in the embrace of a unifying force.

There is no possibility of anything in the universe—a sun, a star, or you and me—existing separately.

To me, this unifying force is the infinite love of the Lord, operating on the physical level. Just as all of us are one, so all things in the created universe are one in the Lord. That is why he is called Vishnu, "he who is everywhere." When the Lord puts his arms around creation so that it can work in harmony, this is love on a cosmic scale. Just as people live together as a family fostering each other's welfare and happiness, the cosmos is a family in which every member is related. If even a distant planet like Neptune or Pluto were removed from the solar system, life here on Earth would be a little different for us all. There is no possibility of anything in the universe—a sun, a star, or you and me—existing separately. Each part derives its significance from the whole, which is what the mystics call the indivisible unity underlying all life.

When Sri Krishna says he is the sun, this can be interpreted with both scientific precision and spiritual wisdom. The sun is the source of heat and light, both of which are necessary for life on Earth. We can ask ourselves, "How has it been possible for the sun to give out this heat and light continuously for more than six thousand million years?" The astronomer and the physicist account for this heat in terms of hydrogen being converted into helium.

With a dramatic touch, they compare the sun to a hydrogen bomb exploding continuously for millions of years. The question that any scientist would ask is, "How is it that these thirteen million degrees at the center of the sun give the perfect temperature for life on Earth?" It cannot be dismissed as an accident. According to the Gita, the sun has an inner law—or, to be more personal, an inner ruler—which maintains a perfect balance of energy, pressure, and temperature. This balance is an expression of the divine unity of existence, which keeps all the local forces working together so that the unity of the solar system may be maintained.

11. ***"Eventually all things fall into place. Until then, laugh at the confusion, live for the moments, and know everything happens for a reason".***

NNK: This insight into the art of facing the chaos of relative existence is from Albert Schweitzer.

'Eventually, all things fall in place' indicates that in the inner journey through the higher dimensions by the practice of surrender or enquiry, one will find the pre-existing point in consciousness where all actions of all beings and their results for all past, and present and future are transcended in that one Supreme Spirit.

'Eventually', itself is a relative word in time and does not exist 'there'. 'There' is a point in space and that too does not exist 'there'. The absolute spirit consumes the infinite journeys of all paths and individuals. No one was ever bound. No one exists who seeks liberation. The 'one' who finds that, loses the separateness from that supreme spirit. Albert Schweitzer says that, in that Supreme Spirit, we are all one, and are sure to find it 'eventually'.

Till then, he gives us three insights into the art of facing the relative life of actions and results (both positive and negative). Laugh at confusion. When the outer life is terribly complex, relax by laughing and by remembering that this intricate chaos is unraveled into non-existence in that one Spirit.

When life appears to be a long affair running into an infinite future having arisen from an infinite past, do not get petrified. Just live for the moment. Moment by moment, live in the understanding that the Supreme Spirit has this apparent limitation; It has to be present in every moment.

As the Supreme Spirit beyond time and space is pure reason, one finally settles all happenings only in pure reason. So, understand that everything happens in the Presence of Pure Reason. Hence the rule 'everything happens for a reason' will bring you relative peace. Living by that rule will 'eventually' unify you with pure reason. In self-enquiry, all three insights are embedded. As each thought arises, do not follow or try to complete it. Enquire, 'For whom is this thought?'. The answer will be, that this thought is for me. Enquire, 'Who am I?'.

DR. MK: Sometimes, life seems to hand out one reversal after another and all that we are doing seems to be falling apart. We may feel that the universe is hostile; we may question the benevolence or even the existence of God.

At such times, it'so important to note that life hasn't always given us a raw deal – we have had things fall in place for us. Whenever we have achieved anything substantial, it was not because of our efforts alone, but also because of many things beyond our control falling in place.

The Bhagavad Gita keeps telling us that even if things are taking a bad turn at present, Krishna is expert enough to bring good out of the bad. If we strive to become conscious of Him by praying to Him, by seeking to take our consciousness to His loving, soothing, sublimating presence, we will realize that the shelter of his remembrance is still available to us. Being reassured by the inner security and serenity coming from our inner absorption in Him, we will realize that things are still in place: He is still in control. This world is a place of dualities, wherein everyone has to go through bad phases; the present is our bad phase.

Just as things have fallen in place in the past, they will fall in place in the future too. We just need to keep plugging on without becoming disheartened.

By thus meditating on the timeless truth that higher than the world's duality stands Krishna's unfailing love, we will, at the very least, not ourselves fall apart when things seem to be falling apart – and thereafter do our part to help things fall in place.

12. ***"Bold is not the act of foolishness but the attribute and inner strength to act when others will not, to move forward not backward."***

NNK: This look at boldness in life is from author and motivational speaker Byron Pulsifer who helps others overcome their failures and face life. He looks at himself in the following way, "During the course of my many careers, I always found that my greatest satisfaction stemmed from helping all people from all walks of life deal with, overcome, and move forward when faced with problems, concerns or self-defeating behaviour."

It is said of Ramana Maharshi and the sages of yore in India that they crossed the turmoil of all the worlds with the support of nothing but inner strength. Inner strength is built through overcoming obstacles and failures by facing them steadily and constantly. Inner strength involves getting up and how many times one may fall. Inner strength is the strength of character built over a lifetime of sacrifice. When this inner strength faces the world or supports a cause, it comes out as boldness and calm strength. So, boldness is not the foolish bravado of someone taking up a challenge on a whim and without the least knowledge about oneself.

In self-enquiry, as each thought is sacrificed in the fire of self-knowledge, the inner strength to know oneself and all the world grows with each thought let go of. The inner strength is complete when all impulses rising from the infinite inner peace and infinite inner strength are erased along with the ego which imagines itself as separate from the limitless inner strength of the source of all. When the peace of the Self meets circumstances, it comes out as inner strength which is real boldness unfazed by challenge.

Dr. MK: Heart attack. Recession. Earthquake. All of us have our fears. Fears that check even choke our energy, making things far more difficult than they need to be. Some people increase their wealth or power, hoping that one day they will become so big that no fear will intimidate them. Sadly, however, that day never comes. No matter how big they become, their bigness is derived from, even dependent upon, external possessions and positions that they can never fully control. So, in a tragic paradox, the bigger they become, the bigger their anxieties become.

To become fear-free and bold, Gita wisdom urges us to become aware of a presence that dwarfs fear – the supreme presence of Krishna.

The Bhagavad Gita in Chapter 16 verse 1 states that fearlessness is the first characteristic of the godly. This fearlessness is a direct result of their godliness or God-consciousness. Krishna presides as the supreme reality in a blissful arena beyond the fear-filled arena of matter. He is bigger than everything – even the biggest problem that life presents. And he makes available his supreme intelligence and grace to all those who seek it by becoming conscious of their eternal loving relationship with him.

13. *"Yātum ūrē yāvarum kēḷir tītum naṉrum piṟar tara vārā"*
"All the places on earth are our town and all the people are our relatives. Bad & Good results do not come from others"

NNK: This overarching look at life as a whole is from the poet Kanian Poongunranar who lived over 300 years before the Christ era. The first line of this poem of Purananuru, a Sangam period (600 - 300 BCE) work in Tamil, is depicted in the United Nations as it reminds us of the common source of all human beings.

All of us have come from the same genetic source. All of us have emerged from the same spiritual source. We are all connected and related. So, every place is 'our' place and each human is our relative. So, it is that one energy of life that is flowing like a river flowing down a mountain. Each one of us is like a log of wood carried by that stream. Whatever good or bad we receive cannot be from others but only due to one's mis adjustment to this flow of life, usually called the power of fate or Grace.

The art of life is to learn to flow. Take death as a common happening and not show undue excitement in relative life offered by the flow of the river. There is no need to praise a great one or look down on an under-achiever as it is all in the flow of life, says the poet in other verses of the poem.

The Buddhist teachings also bring this fact of good and bad results coming through our actions in a scientific way. They show that like and dislike arise from deep within each individual. If one can go to the source of likes and dislikes and live life with a 'witnessing awareness', there is no good or bad in the flow of life. So, ***titum nanrum pirar tara vaara'*** - good and bad do not come from others.

In self-enquiry, one roots out all dualities such as like and dislike by going to their source in the enquiry, 'For whom is like or dislike? Who am I? When the ego is completely rooted out, one directly understands the depth and truth of the words of this poet of the Sangam period.

Dr. MK: Treating everyone and everything equally is a very important life lesson.

It is important to treat everyone equally, irrespective of their region, religion, caste, or creed. It is important to treat people around you like they are your own kin.

It is important to treat different situations in life the same – happiness and sorrow are after all two sides of a coin. Why rejoice at happy events and mull over sad events? Aren't these an integral part of life?

We all know that death is inevitable – why then can we not treat death the same way that we treat life? Don't mourn death.

The power to look at everything objectively, the power to separate your problems, troubles, happiness, and sorrow from 'you' comes from within.

Learn not to be extreme in your emotions – don't idolise a person while you treat another person like trash. In other words, don't be star-struck while looking at Amitabh Bachan, and don't feel superior to a commoner on the street because you perceive yourself as betting better!!!!

Everything is equal in this world – all people, all emotions, all events … if you learn this important lesson, everything becomes simpler. You eliminate most vices that are ruining the world today – bias (based on almost anything – race, religion, gender, region), greed, envy.

14. ***"The body consists of five sheaths and hence all five stand included in the word body. Is there a world independent of a body? Is there anyone who has seen the world without a body".***
NNK: This turn-around enquiry, which changes the very nature of perceiving and tackling our problems in life, is from Ramana Maharshi, a spiritual teacher of the twentieth century, from India.

The five sheaths are the physical body, the breath body, the mind-body, the intellectual body and the 'I' thought. He is turning the problem of life on its head by asking whether without consciousness limiting itself by identifying or attachment to one of these sheaths, is there a world. Has anyone seen any world in deep sleep when all the four other sheaths are lying dormant in the 'I' thought- the root ignorance of not knowing the Self? Tracing the source of the 'I' takes one beyond these sheaths and planes of existence. The implication is that the saviour from all merits and demerits of the world or beings who ever lived, lives now, or who will ever come into existence, is not one who merely lived and died but is a state of consciousness within each one of us here and now.

For whom is this thought? Who am I? This enquiry takes one to that consciousness within, that is beyond all doership. Not only that. The enquiry takes one beyond relative knowing into true knowledge. It takes one beyond relative existence to true existence. Moreover, the problem and solution are brought close to oneself by pointing out that the arising of the separate 'I' is the source of all miseries and erasing that separate 'I' is freedom from all miseries, making the solution direct and independent of outside support.

Dr. MK: In Indian philosophy, the koshas are considered the energetic layers of your body that surround your soul. Sometimes, they're referred to as "sheaths" or "casings." The five koshas exist together and are encased, or nested, within each other. Your physical body composes the outermost layer, while the innermost layer contains your bliss body or soul.

They were first described in the ancient yoga text the ***Taittiriya Upanishad***. This Vedic text is thought to have been written during the sixth century B.C. and provides guidelines relating to spiritual liberation. Some believe the koshas are key to enhancing awareness of your inner world and developing a connection between your mind, body, and spirit. Attention to your koshas may awaken deeper states of awareness on your path to self-realization.

You can visualize the five koshas surrounding the soul as the layers of an onion or a matryoshka — the wooden Russian nesting doll that contains smaller and smaller versions of itself. Working with the koshas may allow you to go deeply into the center of your self or soul. This can help you take your spiritual practice to the next level and make positive changes in your self, your life, and the world around you. An awareness of the physical and mental koshas is the starting point for you to become aware of the deeper layers within.

During the sixth century B.C., the ***Taittiriya Upanishad*** was the first ancient text to discuss the koshas. They were referred to as the five casings that hold the light, purity, and perfection of your true self. The ***Taittiriya Upanishad*** also explains how to develop character and correctly conduct yourself. These ways of living are guidelines on the path that leads to attaining Brahma-jnana, which is the knowledge of your supreme self.

The Viveka Chudamani says, "There is one who is self-existent. He (Self) is manifest all the time in the 'I' thought. Being distinct from the five-fold Kosha (sheath), he is the witness of the three states of experience."

"He" in the above verse refers to the Self. The verse talks about the nature of Awareness. The Self does not depend upon time, place, or any object, and is always available. The "I" notion is dependent on the Self, just like the pot is dependent on the clay.

The Self is witness to the 3 states of experience i.e., waking, dreaming, and sleep. I am neither the waker, dreamer, or sleeper. My real identity is that of the limitless "I", the substrate for everything.

Just as the Self is distinct from the 3 states of experience, it is also distinct from the 5 koshas. No pot is away from the clay, but the clay is distinct from the pot. Similarly, no Kosha is away from the Self, but the Self is distinct from the Koshas.

15. *"We are a way for the cosmos to know itself."*

NNK: This thought connecting the knowledge of the cosmos and knowing oneself is by Carl Sagan, the great scientist who brought science to the common man.

As we are a part of the universe, whatever we have, whatever we know, and whatever we are, belongs to the cosmos. We knowing the cosmos, is the cosmos knowing itself through its thinking part - humans. When we free consciousness from the physical body by detachment, we understand that the cosmos is not merely the sensory cosmos. When we enquire and non-judgmentally look at thoughts, we understand that the cosmos is not merely a flow of energy. Through quantum physics, we come to know that the very act of 'measurement' or 'observing' can and does make the cosmos from a flow of energy to particles or matter. There is no measurement in the cosmos apart from the brain and mind.

Dreams and deep sleep indicate that thoughts can exist relatively detached from the brain. Meditation studies show that consciousness can free itself of brain and thought. In self-attention, one finds that energy that is free of the 'other'. If a human, who is part of the cosmos, is really the self-luminous Self, what else can the cosmos be? Is it merely the matter spread out over time and space? If a human is not the body or matter trapped in time and space, is the cosmos so limited? If a human is not the flow of thought energy divided as 'good' and 'bad' but is unified as one energy in 'witnessing' can the cosmos be the flow of energy through two slits creating a pattern of interference? Is the cosmos not that energy beyond division and interference? Is not knowing oneself, the cosmos knowing itself? Is not self-knowledge, the knowledge of the cosmos? Who am I? Is this a quest merely about the individual? Is not the ultimate truth of the individual also the truth of the cosmos of which that human is a part? As there have been self-realised beings before, is the cosmos a bound existence? Is it not the Self?

Dr. MK: In the early 1980s, astronomer Carl Sagan hosted and narrated a 13-part television series called "Cosmos" that aired on PBS. On the show, Sagan thoroughly explained many science-related topics, including Earth's history, evolution, the origin of life, and the solar system.

"We are a way for the universe to know itself. Some part of our being knows this is where we came from. We long to return. And we can because the cosmos is also within us. We're made of star stuff," Sagan famously stated in one episode.

His statement sums up the fact that the carbon, nitrogen, and oxygen atoms in our bodies, as well as atoms of all other heavy elements, were created in previous generations of stars over 4.5 billion years ago. Because humans and every other animal (as well as most of the matter on Earth) contain these elements, we are literally made of star stuff.

Why God Almighty created the cosmic system... is one question prohibited to be asked by human beings! Bhagavad Gita... the most sacred scripture of Hinduism on Mother Earth prohibits asking this question! Why? It is for the simple reason that the Cosmos exists from time immemorial yet, the Cosmos was created when God Almighty exploded self with a big bang. Imagine a situation in which the collapse of the old cosmos occurs. At this time devoid of all impurities within... the entire Cosmos reduces to the size of half a thumb. And what is this half-a-thumb?

As per the Bhagavad Gita, this half a thumb consists of all purified souls **atmans** in the Cosmos after the collapse of the entire Cosmos. Does this mean at the time of the collapse of the Cosmos (termed **Pralaya** in Hinduism) every soul atman reaches the last manifest stage of life... the 8.4 millionth manifestation... the stage of enlightenment (*kaivalya jnana*). Yes, the truth is so! At the time of dissolution of the Cosmos... all souls **atmans** reach the 8.4 millionth manifestation... finally liberating themselves from the cycle of birth and death forever. Regaining their lost original prime pure pristine primordial form... all purified souls **atmans** occupy the volume of half a thumb!

The moment this cluster of primordial energy we know as God Almighty comes into its original shape... this colossal cosmic power unable to retain itself for long in its prime pure state again explodes with a big bang... resulting in the creation of a new cosmos... a new journey of life! Does this mean the creation of the Cosmos is not in the hands of God Almighty... yes, the truth is so! The moment the big bang occurs... all purified souls **atmans** in their cosmic sojourn hurtle down their cosmic journey at unimaginable speeds. In the melee... hurtling souls' **atmans** gather impurities similar to a rolling ball gathering moss! To cleanse itself of the dross impurities within... every soul atman needs a chain of 8.4 million bodies... and starts the cosmic journey of every soul atman!

16. *"Time and space are modes by which we think and not conditions in which we live"*

NNK: This incredible statement of the world in which we are bound is by Albert Einstein.

Modern science now finds that the 'world' is nothing but reality conditioned by the senses. It is well known that humans have always tried to free themselves of the conditioning of space through travel. Space travel through airplanes and rockets seemed to bring in some freedom from the conditioned existence in space.

Psychologists like Carl Jung show that imagination and dreams show that the psyche is not conditioned by time either. Is the world nothing but reality 'seen', 'smelled', 'heard', 'tasted', and 'touched'? In deep sleep, when the senses are not active and the world is not perceived? However, it is argued that those who are awake when we sleep confirm that the world continues even in our sleep. But, the 'other' who confirms the existence of the world where senses are not active is also seen only when we are bound by our senses. So, that is not enough proof. Senses and the sensory world are thoughts through which the world is perceived and bondage implicitly taken on.

Ramana Maharshi points out that the world and the senses arise only after the mind arises. All other thoughts arise after the 'I' thought arises. So, the 'I' rises from the reality of unconditioned existence-consciousness and ties itself through ignorance in bondage to the thought-speech-body world. The mode to see reality is to go back to the way we came. Self-enquiry takes the 'I' back the way it ignorantly arises and reveals the natural freedom of the Self.

Dr. MK: "Time and space are modes by which we think and not conditions in which we live," Albert Einstein declared in the course of his mind-blowing reconsideration of matter and energy. His work was almost simultaneous with the development of aeronautic science, and it's impossible to think there was no effect of one upon the other. He helped reshape how we think about our temporal presence and convinced us that we are not confined to a place.

Of course, people had long been moving from one place to another before the growth of commercial aerospace – and quite consequentially. The Hebrews moved out of Egypt, and the Persians and Greeks moved armies, as did many others. Marco Polo moved across the known land mass of the world, and Columbus started a new age of exploration. But, even up to the time that the Wright Brothers were redefining aeronautics and Einstein was publishing his new theories on space and time and matter, getting up and moving was an effort and a statement.

In 1923, just to pick a conveniently distant time, making a move similar to one of today's ordinary commercial flights — New York to Los Angeles, or London — was most likely a permanent change. It would consume many weeks or months and was sure to be life-altering. Today, such a flight is barely worth discussing at length. Space does not confine us, and so it does not occupy our thinking or our self-awareness.

And we've conquered space in other significant ways. I can transmit my thoughts to you instantly through various ordinary processes or devices. I can send an image to you so that you have an identical version of the object I am examining. An idea can be converted from my visual impression into a design, and then a draft, and ultimately into a three-dimensional object – from my workspace to a workshop I may never enter, in Los Angeles or London, or anywhere.

I can "be" in your presence with video calling platforms, meaning I don't have to move at all in order to be relocated into your presence. Is it impossible to believe that some further progression of human understanding and engineering will further erode the meaning of "space"?

Let's not worry about what may yet happen. I wasn't alive in 1917 but as Einstein noted I can think about and grasp the understanding of that age. I can appreciate how humans felt a need to be liberated from the confines of space — to go where they are needed or more welcome, to move about as they wish, to live where they can prosper.

But if this is right then Einstein was at least half wrong: "Space" no longer is a mode by which we think, any more than a condition in which we live. Still, "time" remains to define us, and contain us. And that trap may help explain why so many people are offended by emblems of the past, or enraged by indicators of what may yet come, rather than humbled by the impossibly good fortune to be alive today.

17. ***"Life is a process. We are a process. The universe is a process."***
NNK: This observation on life as not being an end but a process, is from Anne Wilson Schaef who is an American Clinical Psychologist and author.

In one sense, Life is a process of unifying. We are in the process of unifying. The universe is a process of unifying spirit. The spirit within my body unifies my body. It loses this strength at the end of the waking state and goes to sleep. Outwardly, like bulbs, each body seems to be separated. But, within each one of us is the unifying spirit. As each thought arises, the 'I' thought seems to be separate from it. But, in spirit, the consciousness within each thought is the same. By asking, 'For whom is this thought? Who am I?', I let go separating and holding the one, unifying spirit within. When this spirit does not find any 'other' apart from itself, it is a self-knowing or self-luminous spirit. This is the One Unifying Spirit within the cosmos. It unifies everything. Nay, it finds nothing apart from itself to unify. It IS.

Dr. MK: What is a process? Well, this is one of those questions that I used to ask myself many times in my life. I have always had questions like "Why are we born?", "Who am I?", "What is the purpose of my life?", "What is the purpose of everything that exists?", "What happens after death?", "What is God?", "What is the limit of the universe?", "Are we alone?", and so on... Then I would try and answer all my questions using my knowledge of science and Hinduism (Vedas, Puranas, etc.).

The history of the universe is a history of motion. This movement from the simple to the complex is built into the web and weave of the universe, and it's called the tendency toward complexity. The tendency toward complexity has carried the universe from almost perfect simplicity to the kind of complexity that we see around us, everywhere we look. The universe is always doing this. It is always moving from the simple to the complex. And we, the humans, are just another instance of this complexity. We're a part of that timeline of this whole getting more complex system, that we call evolution. We're the products of this complexification, and so are the birds, and the bees, and the trees, and the stars, and even the galaxies of stars. And if we were to get wiped out in a cosmic explosion, like an asteroid impact or something, some other expression of our level of complexity would emerge, because that's what the universe does. And this is likely to be going on all over the universe.

As the universe expanded and cooled down, these very tiny bits of things came together to make particles. Then the particles came together to make the first of the atoms. Then the atoms came together to make molecules. Then the molecules came together to make the first of the stars. Those first stars went through their cycles and exploded in a shower of new atoms. The new atoms came together to make more stars and planets. All the stuff we are made of came from those dying stars. We are made out of stars, you and I.

None of these things, none of these processes, none of these coming together actions are what one can describe as random events. The universe has a nature, for and of itself, something like human nature, if you like, and its nature is to combine, to build, and to become more complex. It always does this. If the circumstances are right, bits of matter will always come together to make more complex arrangements. And this fact about the way that our universe works, this moving towards order, and towards combinations of these ordered things, has a name. In Western science, it is called the tendency toward complexity, and it is the way the universe works.

Meditation/Goal

1. *"Men are not prisoners of fate, but only prisoners of their own minds."* ...

NNK: This is a quote from Franklin D Roosevelt. The world and circumstances around us seem so huge and powerful. When one has just lost his job, everything seems to have powerfully conspired to defeat him. The milk is stirred with great care to not spill over and get toppled by the pet cat. We feel that everything is fate.

The law of cause and effect seems so fixed with such an intricate network that we seem compelled to do what we do. Benjamin Libet proves that each action follows a ramping-up time of up to 500 milliseconds before the conscious thought that he finds that none of us have free will. But we find a girl averting her eyes from others and, by this, preventing many diversions to her aim of completing a degree. We see that one decides to study and overcome the temptation to be lazy. Noam Chomsky shows that the ability of human beings to speak 'appropriately', and not out of 'compulsion', in a situation, indicates free will.

So, as Gita points out, the senses are greater than the world, the mind is greater than the senses, the intellect or reason is greater than the mind and the Self is free of all these. As one holds the higher dimension, one can cross the challenges of the lower dimension. So, is man a prisoner of fate? No, but he could remain a prisoner of his mind.

The Maharishi gives self-enquiry to transcend both fate and free will. For whom is fate or free will? Who am I? Self-attention transcends both fate and free will. When self-attention is natural, fate and free will are not.

Dr. MK: In The Bhagavad Gita, chapter 6, verse 34, Arjuna says, *'Chanchalam hi Mana Krishna Pramadee balavadrutam"*. It means 'The mind is very restless, turbulent, strong and obstinate, O Krishna. It appears to me that it is more difficult to control than the wind'. He actually talks for all of us!! He describes the troublesome mind. It is restless because it keeps flitting in different directions, from subject to subject. It is turbulent because it creates upheavals in one's consciousness, in the form of hatred, anger, lust, greed, envy, anxiety, fear, attachment, etc. It is strong because it overpowers the intellect with its vigorous currents and destroys the faculty of discrimination.

The mind is also obstinate because when it catches a harmful thought, it refuses to let go, and continues to ruminate over it again and again, even to the dismay of the intellect. Thus, enumerating its unwholesome characteristics, Arjuna declares that the mind is even more difficult to control than the wind. It is a powerful analogy for, no one can ever think of controlling the mighty wind in the sky. We are what we think and we become slaves to our thoughts – good or bad.

2.   *"Peace of mind is not the absence of conflict from life, but the ability to cope with it."*

NNK: This quote on peace as a presence allowing the whole field of conflict involving relative peace and conflict to exist in it but without affecting it, is from Mahatma Gandhi.

It is clear that we seek peace of mind over and above all other forms of happiness. Sensory and emotional happiness are so fleeting when standing on the ground of a mind that is restless and unsteady. Sri Krishna, in the Gita, points out that whenever the mind is disturbed by a thought, one should withdraw it from that thought and fix it in the Self by holding, 'For whom is this thought?'.

When the mind is naturally self-attentive, it is at peace beyond rest and restlessness. Such peace is not the absence of conflict but complete strength and ability to cope with any situation that comes as a sensory, emotional, mental, or intellectual challenge. Even when one's character or personality is undermined by circumstances or people, one has the peace of mind beyond individuality which is unshakeable by even such challenges of life.

Dr. MK: Peace is a generally much-abused word in our day-to-day life. We don't understand why we use it sometimes. But is peace an antonym of conflict? Well, we can say that disturbing events in our lives make us lose our state of peace. But what does conflict bring? It brings disturbance, irritation, anger, and other negative thoughts and feelings to the fore. But to be peaceful, we must overcome these negative thoughts. We must keep ourselves detached from these. As Sri Krishna says in the Gita, it is attachment with detachment. We do our duties but don't expect or wait for the fruits of it. You had to do your duty and you did. That's all. Don't wait for positive or creditable feedback/results. It might or it might not. Your mind must be detached from this. If you do, then whatever disturbance of conflict happens, you will be able to accept it as a natural consequence and will not be perturbed.

Also, major disturbances like the financial crisis of 2008 or the COVID-19 pandemic of 2020 have brought great trouble to the whole world. Everyone and everything was impacted. But was there anything that you could have done? Apart from being ready to face it. Many of us faced a lot of issues. Loss of jobs, loss of near and dear ones…Yes. All that happens but if we lose our composure and get impacted by these conflicts, then there is no end to troubles.

In verse 66 of chapter 2 of the Bhagavad Gita, Sri Krishna says, *"One who is not connected with the Supreme can have neither transcendental intelligence nor a steady mind, without which there is no possibility of peace. And how can there be any happiness without peace?"*

This is exactly what we need. We need to detach ourselves from the events and get attached to the Higher Self, and not be disturbed or affected by the conflicts.

3. ***"Words have the power to both destroy and heal. When words are both true and kind, they can change our world."***

NNK: Buddha here takes up the question of fate and free will. Is the world predetermined in nature or can it be changed? Buddha says that 'the power of the word' can bring about change in the world. What is it that gives power to those sound waves called words coming from within a conscious human being? The word has to be backed by truth and kindness. These are not dimensions of the sensory world. They are dimensions of consciousness.

Sri Ramakrishna Paramahamsa is said to have asked a mother to come back after 15 days when she asked him to instruct her son not to take jaggery (unrefined sugar) as that habit was causing lots of health issues to the boy. After 15 days, when the boy is brought by the mother, Paramahamsa gives him instructions about stopping the habit. The mother asks him why he did not say these words 15 days back. Sri Ramakrishna responds that he had the habit of taking a little piece of jaggery every day. For 15 days, he abstained from the habit and then the words became infused with truth.

The spoken and written word can be the chisel with which this sensory world atoms are rearranged. So, words have the power to destroy or construct. When truth joins kindness and together, they fill the spoken or written word, the world can indeed be changed. What is the source of truth and kindness? They arise to someone. For whom is this thought about truth and kindness? Who am I? Being the source of words, truth, kindness and the 'I' fills the world with self-attention, and unconditional love. Without a chisel, the sculpture is made perfect. Be still. Fill everything with loving-awareness, kindness-truth.

Dr. MK: Words have the power to make or break lives. So, we should be careful when we speak. Words once out of our mouth, cannot be taken back. ***Tirukkural,*** the famous book of Saint Tiruvalluvar says, ***"Theeyinal sutta pun ullaarum, Aaradhe naavinal sutta vadu".*** The meaning of this couplet is "The wound that is burnt by fire may heal but the wound that is burnt by the tongue can never heal".

Such is the power of words. In The Mahabharata, during the Kurukshetra war, the Pandavas were finding it next to impossible to fight against Drona, who is their Guru. Sri Krishna asked Bheemasena to kill an elephant named Ashwatthama and proclaim that he had killed Ashwatthama. (Drona's son's name is Ashwatthama). Drona could not believe this and asked Yudhishtir if it was true. Yudhishtir said yes. And immediately, his chariot which always used to float a foot above the ground – because he was always truthful and Dharmic - fell with a thud to the ground. See how a lie has such an impact.

4. ***"Don't let the noise of other people's opinions drown out your own inner voice."***

NNK: This quote is from Steve Jobs the co-founder of Apple. In Indian folklore, there is this story of the saint who was taking a rest under a tree in a supine position with a convenient boulder as his pillow. Two village women walking by, remark within his earshot that it is a disgrace that one in a renunciate's robes would still need a worldly luxury like a pillow. The saint thinks this over and removes the convenience. On their way back from their chosen errand the ladies pass by the saint again. Once again, one of them remarks as to what kind of a saint is he if he reacts to the opinions of others!

Moreover, if one looks into one's impulses and prevarications, one can see that there is no 'other person's opinion'. To me, all opinions are filtered by my own impulses and prevarications. I could not understand the advice given by a senior on ethics in 1987. I could not understand what Sri Ramana Maharshi was saying even though I was preparing my daughter thoroughly by going through a book on Ramana and his self-enquiry for her school competition in 1997. But, once I started working on myself, what others were saying, both beneficial and detrimental became clear. So, purify the inner voice. The direct approach to purify the inner voice is to be free of impulses and prevarications. When these arise as thoughts, enquire, 'For whom is this thought? Who am I?"

Dr. MK: This is one of the most quoted quotes of Steve Jobs of Apple. But is it so easy to practically follow? If it is, then all of us would be in pure bliss..is it not? But it can be challenging to do this when you're bombarded by the opinions of others. Whether it's your colleagues, friends, or family, it's easy to get caught up in their perspectives and lose sight of your own inner voice.

So, what can we do to bring it into practice? We should recognize and accept that everyone has their own perspectives and experiences based on which they form opinions. We should also learn to distinguish between valuable constructive feedback/suggestions and unhelpful criticism. We should also have full self-awareness of ourselves. And finally, we must have self-compassion, which will help us to realise that it is ok to make mistakes but we should learn from them.

5.   ***"Truth can be stated in a thousand different ways, yet each one can be true".***

NNK: This provoking idea is from Swamy Vivekananda.

Truth can be approached by letting go of the false, say some. Truth can be approached by holding higher and higher truth, say others. Concentration on something is the appropriate path, say some. Detachment from everything is the truth, say others. Truth is simple, say some. Truth is complex, say others. Be quiet and the truth will come to you. Don't be lazy and be ever-striving, say others. The truth lies in the expanding cosmos, say some. Truth is in the quanta, say others. Truth is in pursuing the differences, say some. Truth arises in conciliation, say others. So, the truth can be stated in different ways.

A spiritual student asks Ramana how to meditate with a mind that is light (**Satva Guna**) sometimes, active (**Rajo Guna**) at other times, and dull (**Tamo Guna**) too many a time. Ramana responds by asking him to go all out in meditation when the mind is light and bear with Rajo and Tamo Gunas. To yet another, for the same question, he asks the student to observe that the mind is light, rushing, or dull and not like or dislike any of those (**Gunas**). To one, he asks to make the best use of the Guna, and to another, he is asking to be beyond Gunas. For whom is truth presented in various ways with each being true? According to my nature, truth appeals to me. Who am I?

Dr. MK: What an interesting observation and saying this is! The truth as we think and say can be multifarious. It can be absolute truth, relative truth, or non-absolute truth. Here's an example of a "non-absolute," or relative truth: "The sky is blue." That may be true—if it's daytime and there aren't any clouds—but the sky won't be the same colour tonight and may not be the same colour tomorrow. And even if it's blue here, it's not blue everywhere. That statement is true, then, in a relative way—relative to time and space. There are unlimited relative truths, but there is only one Absolute Truth. That's why we capitalize the "A" and the "T."

Also, it isn't possible to meditate on relative truths forever. The most pleasant "truths"—if they're not absolute—either stop being true, or you get sick of them after a while. But meditating on the Absolute Truth can make anyone fearless, ecstatic, and always eager for more.

The Maha Bhagavatam Canto 10, Chapter 2, Sloka 26 has this famous verse.

satya-vratam satya-param tri-satyam
satyasya yonim nihitam ca satye
satyasya satyam ṛta-satya-netram
satyātmakam tvām śaraṇam prapannāḥ

The demigods/devotees prayed: O Lord, You never deviate from Your vow, which is always perfect because whatever You decide is perfectly correct and cannot be stopped by anyone. Being present in the three phases of cosmic manifestation — creation, maintenance, and annihilation — You are the Supreme Truth. Indeed, unless one is completely truthful, one cannot achieve Your favor, which therefore cannot be achieved by hypocrites.

You are the active principle, the real truth, in all the ingredients of creation, and therefore You are known as antaryāmī, the inner force. You are equal to everyone, and Your instructions apply to everyone, for all time. You are the beginning of all truth. Therefore, offering our obeisances, we surrender unto You. Kindly give us protection. What a beautiful exposition of The Absolute Truth. He is the real truth and nothing can match that.

6. ***"Health is the greatest gift, contentment the greatest wealth, faithfulness the best relationship."***

NNK: These are the words of Gautama Buddha.

The relationship with one's own body, emotions, and relationships is mindfully looked at by the great teacher. As far as the body is concerned, health is the best gift one can give oneself and others. Always be mindful of the health of the body in food, exercise, and related practices. As far as wealth is concerned, it is contentment that makes one wealthy. As the Stoics point out, it is not how much you have that makes you wealthy. If you want more and more, you are in poverty. If you are content with what you earn and possess, you are the wealthiest person. In human relationships, trust is the key to long happy relationships. Make promises and keep them says Stephen Covey. Long, healthy relationships are the real source of happiness more than even physical health and wealth says a Harvard study on happiness.

Unless one is aware of one's own thoughts, one is merely a slave to thought and is deprived of conscious health, contentment, or building trust. Be aware of each thought as it arises. Enquire, 'For whom is this thought? Who am I?'. This self-attention brings out any hidden impulses from the subconscious into consciousness as a thought. Again, enquire, 'For who is this thought? Who am I?'. Without self-awareness as the underlying truth of life, how can one be naturally mindful of health, contentment, and trust in relationships?

Dr. MK: People are too accustomed to living superficially, without any understanding of the importance of the practice of ethics, that the cultivation of virtues and the disciplining and training of the inner self are entirely neglected. On the one hand, poverty, starvation, and misery, and, on the other, life and sensuous pleasures have played havoc to such an extent that chaos and confusion prevail throughout the world. Here comes the Gautama Buddha, who gave the key to success in this material world and beyond. A sound mind in a sound body, together they are the most useful instruments for the work of the soul. So, naturally, to be born healthy and to preserve that health throughout the soul's sojourn on earth is, indeed, the greatest of gifts.

Similarly, it is very true and correct to accept that contentment is the greatest wealth. In Tamil, there is a saying, **"Podum enra maname pon seyyum marundhu"**.

This means being content with what you have is as good as having gold. That is similar to saying 'enough is as good as a feast'.

And being faithful is nothing more than trusting one another. Buddha says that all the relationships in the world can be sustained by real trust in one another. If members of a family had full trust and confidence in one another, if different communities loved one another on the grounds of common humanity, if nations were not fearful of one another, and if races did not compete with other races, there would be no strife or wars. Faithfulness in relationships should be like a newborn baby. A newborn baby trusts its mother, because the personal self, or the sense of "I", "me", and "mine", have not yet developed. This is simply Altruism.

7. ***"What we call the secret of happiness is no more a secret than our willingness to choose life."***

NNK: These life-affirming words are from Leo Buscaglia, author, professor, and motivational speaker. He was deeply moved during his service as a dentist in the Second World War. The shattered faces he treats deeply touch him. Later, as a professor, he is deeply affected by the suicide of a student. He was the first to state and promote the concept of humanity's need for hugs: 5 to survive, 8 to maintain, and 12 to thrive.

Here he asks us to choose life as the secret to happiness. A customer stands before me at my counter in the Bank. I am adding up pages of numbers. To choose life is to look up from the book and smilingly look at the needs of the customer. I am opening my gate for my afternoon shopping. I see two dogs obviously thirsty in the afternoon sun. To remember the morning paper where someone had pleaded on behalf of birds seeking water in summer is choosing life.

A friend of many years is laid up seriously after a bite from a poisonous insect. To put aside routine and to be there for him is to choose life. When a friend loses his job and feels hopeless, to show that it is an opportunity to look at many options that he had ignored all these years is to choose life. When the mistakes you have committed are overwhelming and the only option seems suicide, to enquire what mistake did the body make; why should I punish the body for what the mind has done? Let me strengthen my mind by meditation and take on life over the next decade. This line of thinking is to choose life. If I, after all this, have hope, everyone surely has hope. Such a thought is to choose life.

When anger arises, not to be caught up but to observe and free oneself of destructive anger or other negative emotions is to choose life. What is the source of anger and action? It is thought. To understand so is to choose life. If I am a slave of thought, my emotions and actions are from bondage to impulses, which is an understanding that chooses life. When a thought arises, to realise that the thought arises as an impulse and not to follow it like a slave is to choose life. To enquire, 'For whom is this thought? Who am I?', is to choose the source of all life and all happiness.

Dr. MK: Everyone wants to be happy, is it not? But is happiness our only goal in life? Well, to think of it, it is not!! Are we at peace, in harmony with the world, doing what we love…these things are more important, come to think of it. Finding something important and meaningful in your life is the most productive use of your time and energy. This is true because every life has problems associated with it and finding meaning in your life will help you sustain the effort needed to overcome the particular problems you face. Thus, we can say that the key to living a good life is not worrying about more things, but rather, thinking about the things that align with your personal values. The key to a good life is caring about only what is true, immediate, and important. The desire for a more positive experience is itself a negative experience. And, paradoxically, the acceptance of one's negative experience is itself a positive experience. Accepting your experience of life as being great and wonderful is the single greatest thing you can do for your happiness.

Albert Camus says, "You will never be happy if you continue to search for what happiness consists of. You will never live if you are looking for the meaning of life.". Problems never stop. They merely get exchanged or upgraded. Happiness is found in solving problems, not avoiding them.

8. ***"Endurance is one of the most difficult disciplines, but it is to the one who endures that the final victory comes."***

NNK: These powerful words on endurance are from the Buddha. The emphasis on endurance is not particular to Buddhism but has a more universal basis in all spiritual paths.

To endure is to suffer something painful or difficult patiently. In other words, patience is one of the most difficult disciplines. At the root of this is the understanding that 'this too shall pass'.

Initially, life poses challenges like waiting your turn in the queue. One learns by staying the course. When the mind wants you to put the book down and go out with a friend, one endures that impulse. One sees the endurance that the space program team under Dr. Abdul Kalam must have had when hundreds of crores and years of effort fell into the sea in a failed take-off. What endurance they must have had to rebuild and succeed a year or so later. One sees the endurance of Satish Dhawan, the chief, addressing the press in failure, to take responsibility, and asking Dr. Kalam, his project head, to face the press when the rocket is a success.

To learn that the three top scientists were each reading from the Gita, the Quran, and the Bible on the morning of the rocket launch makes one learn that endurance can be limitless when one draws from the unknowable, within oneself. One learns that the problem of life and its solution is within oneself. When people all around are talking a different language, holding on to observing oneself and enduring the period of self-observation is difficult indeed. Especially, when friends do not understand your journey and 'pull you' in other directions. To learn that the problem is not outside but in your own attachment to people over principles needs endurance.

When the body and mind are tired and the sick patient is testing you in his suffering, to turn away, to re-gather your energies, and to attend to his needs calls for endurance. As the mind keeps releasing thoughts in an almost endless stream, to hold self-enquiry in seeking the unknowable, limitless source of all, requires endurance. To cross the sea of impulses toward limited goals and abide in the Self is limitless endurance. It is said in the spiritual lore of the Kannada-speaking people of India that there is no greater tapas - penance - than endurance, and patience.

Dr. MK: This quote is attributed to Buddha, though there is another school of thought that says it is not from Buddha but wrongly attributed to him. But the fact of the matter is that endurance is a difficult quality to possess. Very few committed persons have the patience and endurance to stay the course and reach their goals.

I am not a patient person by nature, but it seems like I spend a lot of time waiting. I just hate waiting for the shoes I saw at the mall to go on sale, sitting at red lights, suffering through movie trailers, and watching people in front of me in the check-out line dig through their pockets or wallets for exact change. I can barely tolerate waiting two minutes for a cup of coffee at Starbucks!

Because I lack endurance, I often fall short of the discipline Buddha mentions. My impatient knee-jerk reactions are childish and there is no victory in petty mental temper tantrums.

9. ***"If you are humble nothing will touch you, neither praise nor disgrace, because you know what you are."***

NNK: These simple and profound words are from Mother Teresa.

Humility is the quality of having a modest or low view of one's importance. The more we realise how connected we are with the rest of the creation from the beginning of time and to the limits of space, the more modest is one about one's importance. I am writing this message in English. The linguistics and English language, in one sense, are an evolution of mankind's consciousness over a hundred thousand years. I am merely a spec in that process.

Mother Teresa gets her humility by surrendering to that connecting power of God. She points out, that, if one is arrogant to not take up the role of service, God will find some other deserving speck for the rote. She received high accolades like the Ramon Magsaysay Peace Prize and the Nobel Peace Prize, during her lifetime. Afterward, she was criticised severely as an exploiter of the poor and for advocating spiritual experiences of fighting the darkness till the very end with suffering and feeling disconnected from God. But, to the humble one, who is a nobody under the Omnipotent One, there is no praise to take credit and no disgrace to own. Such a one is obviously beyond praise and disgrace. One knows oneself as a speck serving creation by the power of that one connecting power, God. Such a one serves steadily with peace of mind.

Self-enquiry takes the ego to that undivided connecting power, practically and directly. When the ego is erased at the source, humility is natural in all actions and service rendered unperturbed by praise or disgrace.

Dr. MK: Humility is a quality that our Gurus have been teaching us since time immemorial. Our Puranas have showcased this quality in much splendour. The acme of wisdom is the seat of humility. The wise recognise that the more one knows, the more one realises the immensity of one's ignorance. This is because the supreme consciousness that pervades our existence is infinite. There can be no greater wisdom than experiencing the eternal and infinite supreme consciousness within us. Humility is the prerequisite for learning and growth.

Adi Shankara, in his Soundarya Lahari, beseeches the Mother Goddess with a humble prayer to shower Her Grace through Her glance at all of us. He prays, in the 57th shloka, that he knows he is lowly and far away from Her, and, yet, seeks Her grace. In the second verse of **Subramanya Bhujangam**, he states upfront, again in complete humility, that he knows neither poetry nor prose, knows no great words or their meaning, but what poured forth was the experience of the effulgence of the divine within him.

Hanuman is the epitome of humility in the epic Ramayana. He was virtually an embodiment of all quintessential 'siddhis', powers, and there was nothing that he could not do or achieve. However, he had to be reminded of all that at various stages of the epic as he was not even conscious of it. He was perpetually in a state of experiencing 'Rama bhakti', devotion to Lord Rama. His humility gave him the blessing of being an unparalleled devotee of Lord Rama. Humility is essential for transcending the otherwise impregnable wall of ego, the sense of 'I', which will pave the way for experiencing waves of awareness and truth.

10. ***"True silence is the rest of the mind; it is to the spirit what sleep is to the body, nourishment, and refreshment."***

NNK: These words of contemplation are from William Penn, author, and spiritual thinker of the 17th and 18th Century.

There is a silence of the mouth. This has its value as a penance. Part of the thoughts are at rest. But, the root nature of breath and mind to be moving remains unaddressed. A silent breath or breath that has equalised the outgoing and incoming breaths is deeper silence. It helps quieten emotions and aids even the long-distance runner to allow full use of the strength of limbs without going out of breath.

But it is the silence of the mind that is real silence. Sri Ramana points out that the individual and the world exist in the waking and dream states where the mind exists accessibly and vanishes in deep sleep where the mind does not exist or exists dormant and inaccessible.

So, the silence of the mind quells all disturbances from the world and individuality.

Can the disturbances of mind and world exist without individuality? Still the 'I' in 'Who am I?', and this is real silence. Be Still. This is indeed what sleep is to the body - nourishment and refreshment of the spirit. No; not merely that; when natural and effortless, the silence of the mind is the true liberation of the spirit from its false fetters.

Dr. MK: How often do we let silence into our day and our lives? For many of us, it may be for a couple of moments, at best. Albert Einstein was known to revel in silence, spending hours sitting and pondering. He credited his ability to be quiet as one of the secrets to his success, stating that when he stopped trying so hard and cleared his mind, the answers would make themselves known.

We are a society that takes great pride in "being busy". Sitting, pondering, thinking, being quiet, allowing room for silence … those are activities that no longer seem to fit into the way we live. However, many of us are experiencing greater feelings of anxiety and mental overload. We have so much to do, but yet we are doing it all while running on "empty". To recharge we need to create opportunities to disconnect from constant stimulation and information. Taking time to just be in silence allows our minds to clear away the clutter, process all the input, and make room for ideas and solutions to be generated.

Sri Sri Ravishankar, the spiritual guru keeps saying, 'Just be silent. Observe what happens to your body, and observe the vibrations. Be aware of the mind. What thoughts are going through your mind? Try to detach yourself from these thoughts and let the mind be blank'. Well, this seems to be easy to do, but it is not. The mind is always busy. So, simple silence is the only way we can try to bring the mind to a standstill and give it rest. Shakespeare says, 'Sleep is the death of every day's life'. And it is through sleep that our body rejuvenates itself. In the same way, silence is needed for the mind to energise itself.

11. ***"Happiness can be found in the darkest of times if one only remembers to turn on the light."***

NNK: These words of introspection are from author J.K. Rowling, of Harry Potter series fame, through one of her characters in the series, Dumbledore.

Here the writer is lifting the seeker of happiness from the plane of emotions to the plane of thoughts. By allowing one's circumstances to overwhelm oneself there arises a feeling of terrible misery. The emotions are so strong and depressing that one feels that it is terrible darkness. The author is shifting planes of life when she calls terrible, overwhelming misery darkness. She is asking one to put on the light. The indication is that thoughts can bring in light even in such times. Thought of faith in God. Thought of faith in oneself from past experience. Thought of the good mentors one knows and who are willing to share their knowledge of life.

Thought that we are all connected and the problem of circumstances is merely from an individual life while the power of solving is the one inter-connected life energy that has faced immensely complex problems and evolved. The thought that all of life is together in the subconscious. All the wisdom of one's own culture and the culture of all humanity, as well as spiritual and scientific thoughts of all time, are available to me when I introspect. All such similar thoughts are what the author indicates as bringing light into the darkness. Happiness is a constant companion. For whom is happiness and positive thought a constant companion? Who am I? At the source, there is only self-luminous light. Happiness is not my mere companion. My very nature is natural happiness-unalloyed.

Dr. MK: Happiness is something that people seek to find, yet what defines happiness can vary from one person to the next. Typically, happiness is an emotional state characterized by feelings of joy, satisfaction, contentment, and fulfillment. While happiness has many different definitions, it is often described as involving positive emotions and life satisfaction.

When most people talk about the true meaning of happiness, they might be talking about how they feel in the present moment or referring to a more general sense of how they feel about life overall.

Because happiness tends to be such a broadly defined term, psychologists and other social scientists typically use the term 'subjective well-being' when they talk about this emotional state. Just as it sounds, subjective well-being tends to focus on an individual's overall personal feelings about their life in the present.

Another definition of happiness comes from the ancient philosopher Aristotle, who suggested that happiness is the one human desire, and all other human desires exist as a way to obtain happiness. He believed that there were four levels of happiness: happiness from immediate gratification, from comparison and achievement, from making positive contributions, and from achieving fulfillment.

Does it mean that happy people are ALWAYS happy? No. Not at all. Happy people still feel the whole range of human emotions—anger, frustration, boredom, loneliness, and even sadness—from time to time. But even when faced with discomfort, they have an underlying sense of optimism that things will get better, that they can deal with what is happening, and that they will be able to feel happy again.

It all depends on our mental makeup and attitude. We can, if we want to, be happy. Not letting external influences affect our happy nature. Sri Sathya Sai Baba says, "Always be happy. All I want is your happiness".

12. ***"Everybody wants the truth, but nobody wants to be honest. Everybody is in a hurry, but nobody is on time. Everybody wants to give advice, but nobody wants to listen."***

NNK: This quote of epistemology, tries to study knowledge, and its relationship with reality, just as the subject aims to.

We generally feel that each of us has a different, especially difficult and unique problem. That is probably not true, almost always. We all have the same problem. We want to be happy and do not have the knowledge or practice to find it in this world and relationships.

Here, the quote gives us knowledge as to why we do not find happiness in relationships. We want truth from others but when it comes to being honest with others and oneself, we take a step back. We want everyone to be on time, but though everyone is in a hurry, no one is on time. Why am I not on time? I am not honest with my priorities. I assure a friend that I will be with him for a few hours and then find I have so many other demands for that time. I hurry between my many demands and fail to be on time many times.

I am very good at knowing what works and also share that as advice. But, do I live by what works for all, what is good for all? These are the truths of life that the quote brings before us for enquiry. However, unless I know my mind, how am I going, to be honest, manage various demands on my time and live by the truths I have learned? As each thought arises, without following the thought, let me enquire, for whom is this thought? Who am I? My mind, its prevarications, and its source open up.

Dr. MK: This is one of the things that I keep asking myself many times. The fact is I am always – always means always and not mostly – on time. I am punctual, period. Why? Because I respect time – not only mine but others too. Everyone has the same 24 hours a day. For example, if you are late for a scheduled meeting by 30 minutes, you are not only wasting your 30 minutes, but the other person has also waited for you for those 30 minutes and it is a waste for him too! In all my 38-plus years of professional life, I have NEVER EVER been late for anything. It has been my trait. Punctuality, and discipline have been are ingrained by my parents from childhood and they continue.

Similarly, when you want to be truthful, you need to be honest about it. I read recently that it is difficult to find out the real faces of people. Because, every person has at least three faces – the first one you show to the world, the second one you show to your family and friends, and the third one you never show to anyone. Ironically, we don't know which is the true one! One reason may be that people often fear the consequences of being honest. They may also be worried about hurting others or damaging relationships. Additionally, some people may not be aware of the importance of honesty in their interactions with others. It is important to remember that being honest can lead to stronger and more authentic connections with others, and can help build trust and respect in any relationship.

13. ***"Open your arms to change, but don't let go of your values."***
NNK: This statement of reconciliation between change and constancy is from the Dalai Lama.

Unless there is an acceptance of change, there is no progress. In the outer world, as one learns about life and starts living by the values of life, the circumstances change. One of my students was one of the first batch of recruits through an open examination in a semi-public organization. Having taken the short commission from the Air Force, he was very honest. The environment was full of corruption. But his honesty, at the cost of friction with the beneficiaries, brought about changes in the organisation. He held on. His honesty became deeper when tested and was found not wanting. The system found it too disturbing and moved him to the Global Positioning Implementation team. Here, he was changed from regular corruption of small measure to deeper corruption of life present in relationships. But, the path of progress in understanding life was always in accepting changes on the outside and holding on to values inside.

Buddha, of course, opens up the entire outside world as transitory. Don't expect anything unchanging on the outer, is a value that he wants us to hold within. This brings forth the 'unaffected witness' of ever-present change.

So far as there is the seer-seen relationship, true existence is not experienced, says Ramana Maharshi. In the seer-seen division, consciousness is divided into existence and non-existence. I exist here and do not exist in the object or the medium of perception. The object too exists out there and does not exist in the medium of perception or me. The object perceived, the perception, and the perceiver are apart from each other. Accept this division or change, the existence of subject-perception-object. For Merge them all in the consciousness that is free of division as subject-perception-object.

Dr. MK: Change is the only constant – we keep hearing this regularly. Things around us change which also influences change inside us. The problem is–most people have no idea how to change or what to change. They go in one of two directions, resist all change or embrace all change. Both directions are ridiculous. The first one will turn you into a dinosaur, and the second one will turn you into a jellyfish. The secret is to open your arms to change, but don't let go of your values.

Take your job, for example. Whatever skills got you into your current job may no longer be enough to keep you in that job. Indeed, if you haven't been to several training seminars, read several books, or listened to several audio CDs on professional development lately, you may be in danger of extinction.

It's your values that tell you which changes should be made and how to make them. For example, if you value family, then a change that promises to make you more money but lose time with your family would not be a good change. If you value honesty but your sales manager requires you to say "Whatever it takes to sell the merchandise," then changing to a new job may be necessary. Hold on to your values.

If you value family, but you have to work 70-hour weeks in your job, will you not feel internal stress and conflict? If you don't value competition, and you work in a highly competitive sales environment, are you likely to be satisfied with your job? In these types of situations, understanding your values can really help. Everyone has personal values. Everyone has rules, guidelines, or beliefs that lead their life. Some values come from how one was raised, religion, schooling, or friends. But, even amidst those influences, the values you have are yours.

I recently read a story on values. There was a big-name company looking for a new employee. By the last round of the interview process, only a few applicants remained from the crowd that applied. Through the interview, the company asked the final applicants about their values of honesty and integrity. Each applicant quickly expressed how much they value honesty and integrity.

The applicant was then hired based on one question:

The interviewee was told, "We think you're a really great fit for the company, we are hoping to offer you the position, but first I need to make sure you're right for us."

The company further explained, "You know we're a big company and a lot is going on here. There are some items we receive and send out that we do not put on our reports. Part of your position would require you to come in and oversee the arrival and shipment of those items. Those shipments are not to be mentioned to anyone else. If you would be willing to do that, we will increase your salary by $10,000. Are you willing to do that?"

The first interviewee, excited about the extra cash, replied, "Yeah that won't be a problem!" They told them they'd call him back, after making their final decision on who to hire. He wasn't hired.

The second interviewee was more hesitant about the seemingly illegal operation. The company acted like it was normal to keep items from their reports. He told them he needed to think it over.

By the next morning, he'd concluded that it probably wasn't that bad since it's a big company and they know what they're doing. After telling the company he'd be willing to do it, they told they'd call him back, after making their final decision on who to hire. He wasn't hired.

The third interviewee, when asked, was so confused. He'd thought this company was honest and wasn't sure what to think after hearing about the inside jobs they do and were expecting him to do. He needed a job though.

He asked if he could talk to his wife about it and sleep on it first. Throughout his long, sleepless night, he tossed and turned between his need for a job and his desire to always be honest. He didn't think it would be honest to do what the company was asking him.

After a long, sleepless night, he decided his honesty was most important and he could find a job elsewhere even if it didn't pay as much. He turned down the offer.

Trying harder, the company told him, they really needed him and offered to double his bonus if he'd do it. "I'm sorry, I just, won't do it," was his reply. "So, you're turning down our offer?" the company asked. "Yes, yes I am."

"Well," replied the company, "it is important that we tell you, we don't have any hidden inside jobs like the one we told you about. In reality, we are looking for someone who values honesty and will remain honest even when big money is offered to them. We can see that you are someone whose actions are consistent with their values and we'd like to hire you."

14. ***"Attitude is a choice. Happiness is a choice. Optimism is a choice. Kindness is a choice. Giving is a choice. Respect is a choice. Whatever choice you make, makes you. Choose wisely."***
NNK: These words on free will are from Roy T Bennet, author and inspiring personality who tries to bring the light of positive thought and creative insight in many others.

The argument between free will and fate is never-ending. Without attempting to take that on, the writer is explaining the path to free the will from impulse. He says that, to the one observing his inner world and understanding that the inner world brings love and light to the outer, it is clear that one should be aware of one's inner state.

A positive attitude can be chosen and held only by the witnessing mind. Optimism and giving are not sporadic and compulsive but out of choice to the witness. When one remains an unaffected witness of thoughts, one can choose. Choose wisely. To the one living in the undivided consciousness, the Self, the conflict between free will and fate does not arise.

Dr. MK: You can do what you choose to do. You choose your Attitude, Happiness, Optimism, Kindness, Giving and Respect. Don't let someone boss you around unless it's your parents or your boss from work. This quote is correct for many reasons. It is saying that you can do lots of things without being told to do them. I try to be kind, happy, and giving! Everyone should be! This is saying to be as happy as you can. It will make you feel better.

Many times, we wear a mask to hide our true nature from others. But look at children. They are what they are. They don't hide behind false pretenses. They express their feelings openly without any inhibitions. Can we be like children? It is a choice that we need to make. Whatever choice we make, will define us. There is a saying in Tamil which means ' God and child are one because of their character'. Very true indeed.

15. ***"A child can teach an adult three things: to be happy for no reason, to always be busy with something, and to know how to demand with all his might that which he desires."***

NNK: These words, on the innocence of a child that can teach adults, are by Paulo Coelho, a Brazilian lyricist and novelist.

The key difference between an adult and a child is that the mind of the child is very clear because of innocence. It does not carry hurts, impressions, and images that cloud perception and action. As the mind is clear, it is happy without reason. The adult is happy only when what he likes happens or what he dislikes goes away. The child is always busy as it has not got fixated on areas of interest and disinterest. It is amazed by life and engages with whatever presents itself. Since the mind is without a maze of thoughts, the child, when asking for something that it likes, asks with all its heart. To the adult, so many other thoughts dissipate energy that the demand of what it seeks is lost.

When the mind is made pure and innocent, the adult can be like the innocent child but without its ignorance. The wise man is said to be like a child but free of the ignorance that the child has. When thoughts arise, do not pursue and allow it to cloud your happiness, or dull you, or dissipate your energy. Diligently enquire, 'For whom is this thought? Who am I?'. Return to the original innocence of the source, sans ignorance.

Dr. MK: We have heard 'Child is the father of man' quoted many times. It is indeed an appropriate example of the above quote. Children are innocent, they don't carry any negative feelings or emotions, they forget and forgive easily and hence they teach you so many things. If we can adapt to that kind of attitude with simple needs and simple lives, we will be happy come what may and we will always find something to do. So, a very apt quote indeed.

A child can teach us many things that we seem to have forgotten as we grow – never giving up after a failure, practicing patience, showing and showering unbiased love, expressing feelings, and asking for help. Come to think of it, we do realise that all these characteristics of a child are not difficult to adopt for elders, right? From my personal life, I would like to quote an experience. My granddaughter who just turned five this year had come down from the US after 4 years – a long break due to Covid. We got to spend 2 wonderful weeks with her. The unconditional love that she showered on us is truly unimaginable. My wife and I were in a continuous state of bliss for those two weeks. And I realised the real truth and meaning of this quote.

We seem to grow up forgetting these small things and have been worrying about unimportant things that really don't matter.

16. ***"The highest activity a human being can attain is learning for understanding because to understand is to be free."***

NNK: This philosophical thought on understanding and liberation from bondage is from Baruch Spinoza one of the foremost and seminal thinkers of Enlightenment.

Following Maimonides, Spinoza defined substance as "that which is in itself and is conceived through itself", meaning that it can be understood without any reference to anything external. To him understanding substance or God is freedom. To him, God or substance is caused by itself, conceived by itself, and understood without any reference to anything external. What is, is only God. All other modes of existence exist in God.

To understand oneself as one is, as a limited individual in this substance, is a preliminary understanding of Spinoza. It is one's experience that understanding life makes one understand God or the one substance underlying life. To Ramana Maharshi, the one substance underlying creation is available as the substance underlying individuality. When one starts enquiring 'Who am I?', one starts understanding oneself. But, as the enquiry continues, one understands the 'universal ego' mentioned by Spinoza or the root of individuality. When 'Who am I?', directs the light of enquiry on the 'universal ego' which underlies all objects of creation, the universal ego too is transcended thus crossing the body-mind duality.

Dr. MK: Our Hindu spiritual teachings on Advaita talk about the oneness of *Jeevatma* and *Paramatma*. In The *Vishnu Sahasranama*, sloka 41, it says, *'karanam kaaranam kartha vikartha'*. This means Lord Krishna is the instrument for the creation of the universe; He is the Sole reason and cause for the creation of the universe; Lord Krishna the Actor; Lord Krishna created infinite varieties that filled by the universe; He was the one who cannot be comprehended; Lord Krishna is the one who dwells in the cave of hearts and mind and he conceals everything by illusion He is the instrument, Cause, Executor, Creator, Unpredictable concealer...

When everything is HIM, there is no difference. In the *Lalitha Sahasranama*, it says, *Dhyana Dhyathru Dhyeya roopaya* – the meditation, the meditator and the meditated upon are all Sri Devi herself. Everything being the form of God, there is no distinction. Once you realise this, you are free.

17. ***Bath purifies the body, Meditation purifies the mind, Prayer purifies the soul, Charity purifies wealth, Fasting purifies health and Forgiveness purifies relations.***"

NNK: This meditation on purity is found in all religions and spiritual paths. Cleanliness is next only to godliness is a saying found across almost all cultures. Unadulterated, unalloyed, and uncontaminated are some synonyms of purity. Purity through bathing can be taken to indicate all external cleanliness and order. Bathing purifies the body and orderly placement, dusting and washing keep the external environment pure. More knowledge and application are required to lead a pure life alongside plants, animals, and other occupants of the environment without contaminating the environment and disturbing the ecosystem.

Mind is purified by right living, ethics, and meditation. Prayers, forgiveness, charity, and fasting come naturally to the meditating, pure mind. Mind is pure when it is one energy, undivided. Traditional meditation makes the meditator hold one thought to the exclusion of others till that one thought energy fills the mind. Then, relationships and workflow from that one pure energy. Buddhism asks one to witness away the divisions of thought free of like and dislike. The one energy of unaffected witnessing the mindfulness of Buddhist meditation.

In self-enquiry, the self-attentive energy removes the division even between witness-witnessing-witnessed. The pure 'I-I' fills everything. When that pure energy is held without asking it anything, that too quietens into the pure oneness of the Self.

Dr. MK: In the Jain religion, every year there is a period called '*Paryushan*' at the end of which they say '***Michaami Dukkkadam***'. This means they are seeking forgiveness from everyone. The idea behind it is that - "After requesting forgiveness from all living beings in general as part of **Pratikraman,** I do so one-to-one with you." We become more specific and personal by doing so. In addition to requesting forgiveness, one has to grant forgiveness too. Thus, by forgiving everyone and requesting forgiveness from all we lighten ourselves and our minds from the past year's misdeeds."**Michchhami (Mithya)** means fruitless / forgiven and ***Dukkadam (Dushkrit)*** means bad deeds.

Therefore, the meaning of **Michchhami Dukkadam** is 'My bad deeds be fruitless'. So, the idea behind conveying **Michchhami Dukkadam** is that if I have caused any harm to you, then, may those bad deeds be forgiven, and become fruitless. Revenge is Transient, Only Forgiveness is Complete. We are born to die, and the only thing that Lives through is Forgiveness. To Forgive is a great virtue, Greater than probably any other. Don't see things as we are; See them as they are. Life will be far simpler. Forgiveness is the real form of Love. Forgiveness is understanding that change is inevitable and that it is irredeemable. That is the best way to forget and forgive. To err is human; To forgive is Divine.

18. ***"One who gains strength by overcoming obstacles possesses the only strength which can overcome adversity."***

NNK: This quote on the journey of 'life' is taken from Albert Schweitzer who was an Alsatian polymath. He was a theologian, organist, musicologist, writer, humanitarian, philosopher, and physician. His core philosophy is 'Reverence for life'.

Reverence for Life says that the only thing we are really sure of is that we live and want to go on living. This is something that we share with everything else that lives, from elephants to blades of grass—and, of course, every human being. So, we are brothers and sisters to all living things and owe to all of them the same care and respect, that we wish for ourselves.

It is from out of this philosophy that these words on overcoming obstacles seem to have emerged. Life wants to live. We see a plant sidestep a shading tree and seek light by bending itself, fighting gravity. We see a small pup wag its tail at us, a complete stranger, to win our hearts and that morsel of biscuit, time and time again. Whatever his circumstances, when he sees us on the road, he changes attitude and comes running with great cheer. We find a comrade in arms, from amongst a batch of young officers, who consistently use intelligence, patience, and good sense to reach great heights in the organisation over three decades of consistently facing obstacles, gaining strength, and facing new responsibilities. We find a person, having won materially, faces challenges in dynamic relationships and gaining strength.

We find one who understands relationships and faces the common obstacles of life-death. Such a one finds eternal life. In self-enquiry, with the root problem of birth out of the limitless is addressed constantly. When the 'I' which feels it has been born out of its source and is trapped in a limited mind-body identity, enquires, 'Who am I?', it tackles the root obstacle of all life called death by going beyond the root obstacle called birth. Only the one who is born and separated from the infinite source needs to think of death.

Dr. MK: In the Hindu scriptures, we see that humans can only overcome obstacles by surrendering oneself to the Paramatma. In the Bhagavad Gita, Sri Krishna says to Arjuna in Chapter 18, verse 58,

> *mach-chittah sarva-durgani mat-prasadat tarishyasi*
> *atha chet tvam ahankaran na shroshyasi vinankshyasi*

If you always remember Me, by My Grace, you shall overcome all obstacles and difficulties. But if, due to pride, you do not listen to My advice, you will perish.

Having advised Arjun what to do in the previous verse, Shri Krishna now declares the benefits of following his advice and the repercussions of not following it. The soul should not think that it is in any way independent of God. If we take full shelter of the Lord, with the mind fixed upon him, then by his grace all obstacles and difficulties will be resolved. But if, out of vanity, we disregard the instructions, thinking we know better than the eternal wisdom of God and the scriptures, we will fail to attain the goal of human life, for there is no one superior to God, nor is there any advice better than His.

19.　*'Happiness is a perfume you cannot pour on others without getting a few drops on yourself".*

NNK: This simple yet grand quote is taken from the writings of Ralph Waldo Emerson considered to be one of the pillars of the growth and wealth of the United States by deeply influencing American thought. He led the transcendentalist movement in the mid-nineteenth century. The core of the transcendental philosophy is that happiness is inherent in man. They believed in the goodness of the individual. It is easy to see how the quote emerges in such a great mind.

When the understanding is that happiness is inherent in the individual, it is obvious that one cannot bring happiness to others except with a few drops of that perfume falling on oneself. One can imagine the welcoming team in an Indian Wedding. The lovely youngsters keep perfume bottles in their hands and sprinkle on all invitees. The wind and atmosphere ensure that some part of those fine particles of perfume fall continuously on those youngsters too. However, the transcendentalists believe, relying on the teachings of the Upanishads along with their discussions deep into the nights in Walden Pond, the residence of Emerson, that the individual is essentially good and not merely getting a few drops of happiness while giving happiness to others. What is the fountainhead for this inherent happiness? The Upanishads say that one's essential nature is existence-consciousness-bliss. It is a happiness that is conscious and ever-present.

Ramana Maharshi shows that everyone enjoys this happiness in deep sleep where there is no mind. So, when the mind originates as thought, we move away from our Natural Happiness by following thought. When a thought arises or a mind arises, He says that one should not follow that thought and move away from Natural Happiness. But, one should with diligence enquire, 'For whom is this thought? This thought is for me. Who am I?' By stilling the 'I' one returns to one's source, the natural, unalloyed happiness. When the impulse to follow thought is completely erased, the ego nature is erased and one abides in one's natural happiness; existence-consciousness-bliss.

Dr. MK: The first meaning of this quote by Ralph Waldo Emerson speaks about the joy of sharing happiness with others. We can perhaps challenge this – there is also a thing called selfish happiness! No matter how much we like to believe that we're isolated characters and completely independent, we're connected. There is a special sense of joy when you do something for someone else apart from you.

Some people may call it selflessness, but if it makes us happy – then maybe it is selfish too. I don't want to get into the semantics, but the purpose of life is to be happy, right? And everyone wants to be happy. And that means, giving ourselves all opportunities to be happy. If you stop for a minute and ask yourself – how can I be happier? you'll start finding some amazing answers. Maybe to extend it a bit more, we can infuse it with love, kindness, and happiness for others. It is one of those things that gives you double the joy as you share.

Making someone else happy, gives us a sense of warmth and joy that sparks a bit of magic within us. I want to share a small anecdote that happened years ago but made me smile.

A cute little story came to my mind. It was the time for evening snacks and all were eating the cake which was distributed equally among all. A young kid, after finishing his piece of cake tried taking a little from the girl next to him. Being a bit reluctant, the kid went away but after some time the same girl came toward him offering her share.

It took me by surprise and I asked her *"You don't have a cake now, are you not sad?"* The girl replied "He is happy" and I asked "You?" and she said, "Of course, I am happy". Maybe it was the innocence of her face or the sheer joy in her smile that swept me away that day. But I couldn't help myself reminiscing about this incident. Tiny droplets of joy, aren't they?

Happiness is reciprocal. You make someone happy and you are happy, either by them or by the act of making them happy. It may be a little out of comfort to make others happy at times. But more often the effort, money, time, and energy spent will always be rewarded with much more happiness than expected. And who doesn't like such rewards?

20. *"Through meditation and by giving full attention to one thing at a time, we can learn to direct attention where we choose."*

NNK: This quote on meditative living is from Eknath Easwaran who was an Indian-born spiritual teacher, author translator, and interpreter of Indian religious texts such as the Bhagavad Gita and the Upanishads.

Easwaran developed a method of meditation – silent repetition in the mind of memorized inspirational passages from the world's major religious and spiritual traditions – which later came to be known as Passage Meditation.

There is an incident in the life of Ramana Maharshi. Once the Ashram had grown and food had to be prepared for many, Ramana would join in with others in the kitchen to cut vegetables beginning at around four in the morning. Once, an ardent practitioner of self-enquiry who was a disciple of Ramana by the name Kunju Swamy was in the team of vegetable cutters. He was looking up at the clock time and again. Ramana looked up and asked why Kunju Swamy was looking at the clock. The disciple responded that he felt this time could have been better spent in the meditation hall, doing self-enquiry. Ramana responded that, probably, he would get thoughts of vegetable cutting there. The suggestion was to do the present job, observing that no other thoughts, including the thought of self-enquiry, were allowed to intrude. A gentle observation of the act of washing vessels is turned into self-enquiry when one observes the other thoughts that try to enter and lets them go, gently holding on to the task in the mind. One can be self-attentive while doing the task on hand with all attention. When one is free of other duties, one can do self-enquiry without the support of the one thought of the task at hand.

Dr. MK: In Chapter 6 of the Bhagavad Gita, Krishna describes the Practice of Meditation:

"Those who aspire to the state of yoga should seek the Self in inner solitude through meditation. With body and mind controlled they should constantly practice one-pointedness, free from expectations and attachment to material possessions. Arjuna, those who eat too much or eat too little, who sleep too much or sleep too little, will not succeed in meditation. But those who are temperate in eating and sleeping, work and recreation, will come to the end of sorrow through meditation. Through constant effort, they learn to withdraw the mind from selfish cravings and absorb it in the Self. Thus, they attain the state of union."

When meditation is mastered, the mind is unwavering like the flame of a lamp in a windless place. In the still mind, in the depths of meditation, the Self reveals itself. Beholding the Self utilizing the Self, an aspirant knows the joy and peace of complete fulfillment. Having attained that abiding joy beyond the senses, revealed in the still mind, they never swerve from the eternal truth. They desire nothing else and cannot be shaken by the heaviest burden of sorrow.

The practice of meditation frees one from all affliction. This is the path of yoga. Follow it with determination and sustained enthusiasm. Renouncing wholeheartedly all selfish desires and expectations, use your will to control the senses. Little by little, through patience and repeated effort, the mind will become still in the Self.

In Chapter 6 Sri Krishna says, "Whenever the mind wanders, restless and diffuse in its search for satisfaction without, lead it within; train it to rest in the Self. Abiding joy comes to those who still the mind. Freeing themselves from the taint of self-will, with their consciousness unified, they become one with Brahman."

21. *"Meditation is the dissolution of thoughts in Eternal awareness or Pure consciousness without objectification, knowing without thinking, merging finitude in infinity".*

NNK: This all-encompassing look on Meditation is by Voltaire who was a French Enlightenment writer, philosopher, and historian.

Thoughts appear and disappear. Thoughts have tremendous energy to connect or disconnect. Thoughts have the energy of like and dislike. Thoughts can keep one in heaven or hell, albeit for limited periods. To cross the alternating of life between heaven and hell, one has to look beyond thought. From where do thoughts arise? Trace the source of any thought in Meditation. There will be the 'I' thought at the root. All thoughts arise for the 'I'. Other thoughts and their existence are known to the 'I'. The 'I' thought does not need the support of any other thought to know 'I exist'. This fragrance of self-awareness is the sample of the fragrance of the infinite consciousness which will not need the support of any other object to know its eternal existence. So, meditation is the dissolution of thoughts in that infinite awareness. In one sense, one brings that freedom into this relative existence, knowing without thinking. In another sense, there is no finite plane left for the infinite to be brought. This is the merging of the finitude into infinity.

Dr. MK: This quote is also attributed to Swami Sivananda. Meditation is an intense spiritual as well as personal experience. Meditation may be described as a state of concentrated attention on a thought or on awareness. This thought process is, to turn the attention inward, to the mind itself. Meditation is used for personal development, better concentration, to achieve peace and harmony, spiritual closeness to God, to become healthier and even to impart calmness, love, purity, well-being, and truthfulness.

One of the meanings of the word meditation is to control the activities of the mind, speech, and body. Steadying the mind or focusing the concentration is one of the prime objectives of meditation. Once the attention gets intermeshed then concentration slowly turns into meditation or dhyana. It is then that the person who effortlessly merges with the object of concentration, which might either be the present moment or could be the Divine Entity.

Meditation is the path to attain closeness to one's soul. Meditation cleanses the soul from within and this change can be seen physically in a person, from outside.

22. ***"Maxim for life: You get treated in life the way you teach people to treat you."***

NNK: This meditation on the strength of reactions is by Dr. Wayne W. Dyer who was a self-help author and motivational speaker. He has done a deep study on the power of thought energy and found solutions for practical living through observation of oneself. The whole quote is, "How people treat you is their karma; how you react is yours. Maxim for life: You get treated in life the way you teach people to treat you. If you change the way you look at things, the things you look at change. When you judge another, you do not define them, you define yourself."

To react to another merely affirms the behaviour of the other. When we do not react to another, it is not only that we are free of our karma, we also bring a fundamental change in the other. While walking in the marketplace, Buddha is severely abused by a young man. He does not react at all. After some time, his disciple asks him why he did not correct the erring youth. Buddha points out that if someone gives a gift and you do not receive it, the gift remains with the giver. The anger and abuse remain with the abuser. That pain will correct him.

Here, Wayne W. Dyer is pointing out that if one does not judge in the present moment, the good or bad that others give, their karma remains with them. This shall correct them. This shall eventually change how they treat you. When you judge another, you are not defining them but you are defining yourself. Living in the present beyond judgement is freedom from one's own karma. This is the practical application of Buddhist thought.

To be free of judgement, one should be free of impulses or vasanas which push the ego into judgement. In self-enquiry, the ego is taken to its source and merged with the Self. There is no impulse to correct another, even indirectly. The depth of the subconscious where one does not judge others is not only found and understood but, the whole of the subconscious mind is understood and transcended in self-enquiry.

Dr. MK: The *golden rule* is a moral principle that denotes that you should treat others the way you want to be treated yourself. For example, the golden rule means that if you want people to treat you with respect, then you should treat them with respect too.

The golden rule is an important philosophical principle, which has been formulated in various ways by many different groups throughout history, and which can be used to guide your actions in a variety of situations. As such, in the following article, you will learn more about the golden rule, see how it can be refined, and understand how you can implement it in practice.

Different people tend to be exposed to different forms of the golden rule to a different degree, based on factors such as the predominant religion in their society. However, all these forms of the golden rule revolve around the same underlying concept and around the same underlying intention. Namely, all forms of the golden rule aim to help you treat others better, by using the way you yourself would want to be treated as a guide of how to behave.

Teaching people how you want to be treated starts with yourself. You may need to first define what works and doesn't work for you. Then, you can be transparent with others.

Teaching others about what you want doesn't guarantee they'll follow suit, though. So, it may also be important to learn how to let go of things you cannot control.

Teaching people how to treat you is a process that involves introducing them to "what is acceptable and unacceptable. It is knowing what we need and want, and being able to communicate it effectively to others,"

You either teach people to treat you with dignity and respect, or you don't. This means you are partly responsible for the mistreatment that you get at the hands of someone else. You shape others' behaviour when you teach them what they can get away with and what they cannot.

If the people in your life treat you in an undesirable way, figure out what you are doing to reinforce, elicit, or allow that treatment. Identify the payoffs you may be giving someone in response to any negative behaviour. For example, when people are aggressive, bossy, or controlling — and then get their way — you have rewarded them for unacceptable behaviour.

23. *"A man can surely do what he wills to do, but cannot determine what he wills. Fate and free will are equally powerful forces but I consider free will to be more important as it is your free will that determines your fate. We must believe in free will - we have no choice."*

NNK: This enquiry into one of the deepest topics of philosophy and spirituality is by Stephen Hawking, arguably the greatest scientist of our time. In an article entitled 'Is everything determined', he concludes that, of course, it is. However, it might as well not be as no one can ever know what is predetermined.

If the survival of the human species is considered a worthy subtitle under 'everything is pre-determined', then it is necessary that we hold free will accountable. Unless the aggression of our DNA from animal ancestors is transcended by introspection and care of the intellect, humans are bound to destroy themselves. Nuclear power coupled with the aggression of reptilian ancestors will go only one way unless the free-will can be guided to peace.

Here, in this quote, he points out that though a man can surely do what he wills, he cannot determine what he wills. His thoughts from the subconscious are themselves conditioned. However, we must believe in free will if we value human life. In self-enquiry, one seeks the source of both free will and fate by holding the 'I'. When the conditioned 'I' falls away, both free will and fate fall away. Such a one will not fall into arguments about which is more powerful.

Dr. MK: In Chapter 5, Verse 15, of The Gita, we clearly see that God has given free will to all individuals and explains the relationship between the concept of The Lord's doership and free will clearly.

nādatte kasyachit pāpaṁ na chaiva sukṛitaṁ vibhuḥ |
ajñānenāvṛitaṁ jñānaṁ tena muhyanti jantavaḥ

The omnipresent God does not involve Himself in the sinful or virtuous deeds of anyone. The living entities are deluded because their inner knowledge is covered by ignorance.

God is not responsible either for anyone's virtuous deeds or sinful actions. God's work in this regard is threefold: 1) He provides the soul with the power to act. 2) Once we have performed actions with the power supplied to us, He notes our actions. 3) He gives us the results of our karmas.

The individual soul has the freedom to perform good or bad actions by the exercise of its own free will. That free will is the basis of the play of creation and it accounts for the varieties of consciousness amongst the souls in existence. God's work is like that of an umpire in a cricket match. He keeps giving the results, "Four runs!" "Six runs!" "He's out!" The umpire cannot be blamed for the decision, for it was based on the way the player performed.

One may ask why God granted free will to the soul. It is because the soul is a tiny part of God and it possesses His qualities to a minuscule extent. God is **abhijña swarāṭ** (supremely independent), and so the soul also possesses a tiny amount of independence to utilize its senses, mind, and intellect in the manner it wishes.

24. *"I do not believe in free will. Schopenhauer's words: 'Man can do what he wants, but he cannot will what he wills,' accompany me in all situations throughout my life and reconcile me with the actions of others, even if they are rather painful to me. This awareness of the lack of free will keeps me from taking myself and my fellow men too seriously as acting and deciding individuals, and from losing my temper."*

This art of living using determinism or lack of free will is by Albert Einstein. He agrees with Schopenhauer that each one can do what he wants but cannot will what he wills. So, in action, I am as bound as the next man. But I have freedom in my inner acceptance of the actions of others and review of my actions. Here, if I practice surrender to predetermination, I can remain peaceful about my actions on review and of others' actions even as they happen. This brings a non-reactive dimension beyond deterministic actions.

In self-enquiry, one looks at thoughts and learns the art of letting them go. One can see how Schopenhauer and Einstein are practical. One goes deeper as one observes one's own thoughts and lets them go. The subconscious that determined the will is now brought to light. One cannot 'claim' this freedom as that would mean being struck in the area of action and approval by others. But, the inner freedom from a determined will is also deepened and transcended when the ego is erased. One sees the practical living of Einstein and goes beyond to a deeper peace where one's ego and the first pre-determined push of the ego are taken to their source. One can practically see the combined will of all. playing out with inner peace. The inner peace or consciousness envelops and transcends the plane of actions as the self-luminous Self.

Dr. MK: "Now I have become Time, Destroyer of worlds!", says Sri Krishna to Arjuna in that apocalyptic scene of the Bhagavad Gita when He shows him His awesome and terrifying Universal Form. The concept of fate and free will in the Mahabharata is deep and complex like the epic itself. The Mahabharata itself seems to support the concept that the Great War was predestined.

This theme resonates in the Mahabharata. Lord Krishna, Vyasa, Narada, and other great rishis knew that the great catastrophe was predestined. For instance, Vyasa advises Satyavati, Amba, and Ambalika that they should retire to the forest after the death of Pandu, as otherwise, they would be witnesses to the suicide of their race. Draupadi is referred to as being born for the destruction of the Kauravas and Kshatriyas. In the Vana Parva, Shri Krishna assures Draupadi that the earth would drink the blood of the Kauravas in a future catastrophic war. It is as if Lord Krishna was conducting a sacrifice of war in which all the Kshatriyas of the world would be annihilated. But what was the secret behind this planned destruction of the Kshatriyas?

Thus, as in Life itself, Fate and Free Will form the two strands that weave the rich tapestry of the Epic. The spirit of the Mahabharata however is not fatalistic. Vyasa's vision is reflected in the action-packed life of Shri Krishna, the supreme hero of the epic. The great poem reverberates with His grand personality and inspires us to be like Him- mighty and full of courage, never disheartened and ever enthusiastic, ready to crush evil and establish Virtue on earth. And isn't Arjuna's annihilation of the Khandava forest with Krishna's help an illustration of man's ability to destroy the forest of self-limitations with God's grace and achieve high goals by self-exertion? The heroes of the Mahabharata are the great karmayogis: Bhishma, Karna, Krishna, and Arjuna, and not the dubious fatalist Dhritarashtra.

25. *"Find Joy in discovering what makes your soul happy."*

NNK: This is a quote doing its rounds on the internet with source not known.

Ramana Maharshi in the preamble to the work, 'Who am I?' brings out a fact of philosophy - that everyone seeks only happiness.

All living beings desire to be happy always, without any misery. In everyone, there is observed supreme love for oneself. And happiness alone is the cause of love. In order therefore, to gain that happiness which is one's nature and which is experienced in the state of deep sleep, where there is no mind, one should know oneself. To achieve this, the Path of Knowledge, the enquiry in the form of "Who am I?", is the principal means.

It is the finding of Behavioural Psychology that people are not creatures of reason. Most of the decisions are made without logic. So, this fundamental fact of philosophy lies hidden from the unenquiring human. We feel we are seeking a better house, a better bank balance, a better relationship, and so on. But essentially, we seek happiness. This happiness is within us and not outside. In deep sleep, where there is no mind, everyone enjoys this natural happiness. To bring out this happiness, one has to go beyond mind - thought - here and now. When all thoughts, including the root thought 'I' are transcended, the unconditional love, unconditional, unalloyed happiness of the Self IS.

Dr. MK: We spend our lives chasing happiness. However, we often end up distracted and looking for it in the wrong places. Corporations convince us to buy things that we don't need, to impress people that we don't even like. And we work in jobs we hate, to make money that we think will bring us happiness.

Every living creature wants to be happy. Whether it is money, power, or something else, you seek it for the sake of happiness. Some people even seem to enjoy misery because it gives them happiness! To be happy, you seek something. But despite getting it, you are not happy. A schoolboy thinks that if he goes to college, he will be more independent, free, and, therefore, happy. When you ask a college student whether he is happy, he feels that if he gets a job, he will be happy. Talk to somebody who is settled in his job or business, and you may find that he is waiting to get a perfect soul mate to be happy. Then what? When he gets a soul mate, he now wants a child, to be happy. Ask those who have children, if they are happy. They respond that how can they relax until the children have grown up, have had a good education, and are successfully settled on their own? Ask those who are retired if they are happy. They long for the days when they were younger.

How to make your soul happy? Some tips – make some personal time every day for yourself, learn to relax, be positive, and treat yourself to small wins. Most importantly, subdue your ego. Ego can destroy your tranquility. Once a man asked a scholar "I want happiness". He replied; first, remove 'I' That's EGO. Then remove "Wants". That's "desire". See now you are left with only "happiness". A happy soul can never be Egotistic. Be a happy soul & fix your life. You need to understand that life is what you create or discover. It isn't a piece of cake. You were given this life because you are strong enough to live it.

26. ***"In every adversity there lies the seed of an equivalent advantage. In every defeat is a lesson showing you how to win the victory next time."***

NNK: These are the words of Robert Collier who was an American author of self-help and New Thought metaphysical books in the twentieth century.

One fails an exam for entry into banks. One can brood over the adversity all life and suffer or take it as a learning opportunity to find out one's weakness in reasoning, math, or English and rectify it. In making life a series of opportunities to learn, one comes upon a deep adversity that no friends or relatives can solve. One goes to the root of the adversity and comes upon the root problem faced by all living beings in relative existence. One works on that adversity and learns about **Karma, Bhakti, or Buddhi** Yogas. One learns that the Supreme present within each one is putting each relative being through adversity only to teach about yoga or union with the Supreme. As Sri Krishna says, those who have simple faith and constant meditation of Me, I give their Buddhi the humility to merge into the Supreme Self.

So, not only does adversity hold the seed of learning and advantage, but when one takes up the greatest adversity of birth and death, there is learning of Yoga with the Supreme. So, every adversity indeed has the seed of an EQUIVALENT advantage. Take up the root problem faced by all living beings. You will struggle. But surely, Truth is bound to reveal itself.

Dr. MK: The level of uncertainty in business and in life is rising around the world, or is it? Did we ever really have certainty about the future? We made plans and we made contingency plans but many of us never planned for this. How can we continue to achieve our goals in business and in life? How do we begin to overcome the challenges we are facing and how do we help our employees do the same?

One quote from Napoleon Hill describes a positive perspective in answering some of these questions:

Every adversity, every failure, every heartache carries with it the seed of an equal or greater benefit.

Some sources quote Hill replacing "benefit" with "opportunity". What can we learn from every obstacle we are facing and are we going to allow this adversity to improve our strengths or limit us? What good can we find in this? What opportunities are being placed before us today?

You might be feeling powerless over your circumstances, but you have power over your attitude and your actions. These will determine your success or failure – that is one thing that is certain.

Attitude is the lens through which we choose to see the world. We can choose to feel overwhelmed and then become defeated or we can choose to adapt our strategy to the current environment. We can be stagnant or creative. We can stand stunned like a deer in headlights or move forward. What do you choose?

When faced with a crisis, it can be difficult at that moment, to imagine the experience will eventually lead to some type of growth. Resilience is a person's ability to bounce back from adversity and grow from the challenge, and research now shows that past adversity can help you persevere in the face of current stress.

Adversity makes you stronger – by increasing empathy, by triggering post-traumatic growth, by building self-efficacy, by helping you to find the real good, and by enabling us to convert stress into challenge.

Adoration/Love

1. *"You will never be happy if you continue to search for what happiness consists of. You will never live if you are looking for the meaning of life."* ...

NNK: This is a quote from Albert Camus, French Philosopher and Nobel Laureate.

When we see luscious mangoes, the senses and mind make us feel that happiness is in possessing and consuming the mango. But Reason points out that those who undertake intermittent fasting or regular fasting for long periods or control their diet for decades to face juvenile diabetes have happiness that is beyond sensory consumption or non-consumption.

A person who opts for the right action and right thinking, through consistent practice in day-to-day living, gets the identity that 'I am a good person' and has happiness that cannot be touched by sensory deprivation of concentration camps or lack of education as the identity is established with repeated victory over senses, mind, and intellect. But even such happiness can be undermined by someone who points out the inability of that person to be present always.

The challenge about the good person not being available to carry out the right action could be from a dependent who points out that you were not available in a crisis. Only by going beyond individuality in self-inquiry, can one find the Brahmananda or Atmananda from within, which then permeates everything.

So far as I identify with my lower or measurable selves - body, breath, mind, and intellect - I limit myself and am subject to desiring something outside me. In finding the source of the ego, one finally transcends desire - the root obstruction to natural happiness. To such a one, there is no search for happiness or meaning of life outside oneself.

Dr. MK: In The Ramayana in Sundara Kandam, Saint Valmiki talks about Sri Hanuman lamenting about Ravana. Hanuman sees Ravana for the first time and says, *"Aho Rupam, Aho Dhairyam, Aho Satvam,*

Aho Dhyuti... " He was impressed by the personality, power radiating from Ravana's eyes, and his valour and then says, "If only he had not succumbed to the sin of abducting Sita Mata, he might have even ruled the three worlds". Ravana's greed, desire, and acts against Dharma eventually led to his downfall. He was looking at sensory happiness which caused his death.

Happiness is a state of mind. There is a popular anecdote of Sundar Pichai, CEO of Google, talking about happiness. He says, "Happiness is like a butterfly. If you keep running after it, it will fly away. But if you sit quietly, the butterfly will come sit on your shoulders".

2. ***"Your beliefs become your thoughts. Your thoughts become your words. Your words become your actions. Your actions become your habits. Your habits become your values."***

NNK: What is realised by introspection is also learned through the cycle of experiences and interactions with the world of objects, people, and relationships. Gandhiji is giving an overview of this external learning cycle. What is a belief, let us say, 'speaking truth makes me purer', becomes a thought. I start speaking about what is truth to me. I have to carry out what I speak. So, my actions started becoming ethical. Speaking the truth and acting ethically become habits. This habit leads to the reforming of values inside.

Could I not learn values and ethics directly by introspection on life learned from reading and listening? Surely, this introspection quickens the external learning cycle. Is the source of ethics in the world or within me? The source of ethics is sought within. The cycle of learning on the outside and in introspection is completely understood.

Who am I who acts ethically and speaks the truth? Am I separate from my source? Is any individual separate from the source and others? Who am I who feels there is learning from outside and from within? For whom is this division of the external cycle and introspection cycle? Who am I? The undivided consciousness reveals itself to the one who lives in the true understanding of external and internal learning.

Dr. MK: Let us look at how children learn. They observe parents' and elders' behaviour. They think what the elders do is right. They put it into action and over some time, action becomes their habit. For example, if the child keeps hearing negative, angry words at home and sees the parents fighting and arguing, it might start feeling that it is the right behaviour.

Over a period of time, the child starts behaving aggressively and violently thinking that it is natural as it has seen parents do the same!! Child psychologists agree that this is a major reason for the kids' change in behaviour. So, we should be very careful of what we speak and do in front of our children.

3. ***"Accept the things to which fate binds you, and love the people with whom fate brings you together, but do so with all your heart."***

NNK: This thought is from Marcus Aurelius, the great Stoic.

We may be given by a democratic election, a rude shock by the people selecting a team not liked by us. Artificial Intelligence may grow exponentially and almost all intellectuals may indicate a period of loss of jobs and a shrinking of the demand cycle. However, if one can embrace what fate has brought, one has a clear mind to deal with life.

How to accept fate? When we look back at life, we find that when we have lived attentively, accepting fate as it comes, one has lived and learned. When we have depended on circumstances, periods of adversity have uplifted us ultimately while comfortable periods have brought laziness, to say the least. The Covid years were years of severe adversity for the whole world. It brought losses of no small order. But going through this period together, humanity has uplifted itself. We learned that we can act together without waiting for a common adversity. Our health delivery systems improved by leaps and bounds when limits were tested. Many limits were tested and expanded, surprisingly many times. The human character showed a deeper strength as doctors, nurses, businessmen, bankers, and many others put their lives at stake for others.

One now gears up to make the best of an unfavourable (in one's opinion) government or challenging technology. The consciousness within is untouched or untrammeled by fate. One not merely cooperates with what fate brings but does so with all one's heart!

Dr. MK: It also brings to our attention how we are linked by fate. I fondly recall the meeting with Nandu (co-author of this book) in Madurai Meenakshi temple on the 14th of July 2014. Both my wife and I were standing in the queue for the darshan of Meenakshi Amman and there he was calling me, 'Murali, Murali'… Remember that we had not met for more than 2 decades before that. The moment we met we were able to recognize each other and it was a pleasurable interaction for more than half an hour. It rekindled our relationship and the result is what you are seeing now, co-contributors to this maiden book from us. How did he come to Madurai on the same day? Why should we be there at the same time at the same place? How did he recognize me after so many years? Can we find logical answers to these and other questions? I am sure not.

It is HIS wish that we should meet that day in the sanctum sanctorum of Devi. It is all HIS doing. People may call it fate, chance, or anything else. But the other day when Nandu and I were chatting about the incident, I really became emotional. How does God decide whom to bring into one's life? How HE makes things happen. It is for us to just accept HIS direction and go with the flow. People come into our lives for a reason. We meet people for a reason. Even in a train or a flight, we come across so many co-passengers. Not all of them will even have a chance to meet again. But some of them we may continue to relate to. They are meant to be a part of our life. We have to accept that.

4. ***"The greatest part of our happiness depends on our dispositions, not our circumstances."***

NNK: This great thought on inner dispositions bringing happiness rather than circumstances is from Martha Washington, the first First Lady of the United States of America.

The humility of the person is manifest in the way in which she has maintained a probabilistic approach to her words. 'The greatest part of happiness', indicates her understanding that absolute happiness is not explainable. We normally take happiness to be a product of circumstances. A happy occasion comes about and one feels happy. But, the mind forgets this and gets back to what it is usually disposed to. A generally angry person continues to be angry and a generally doubtful person continues to be so. So, the First Lady is suggesting that one work on one's disposition or *'guna'*, as Sri Krishna puts it.

If one has an accepting and grateful disposition, one finds the ability to be happy irrespective of circumstances. Sri Ramana Maharshi, of course, says that one's very nature is happiness. In deep sleep, where there is no mind, each one experiences this natural happiness. To make that one's natural disposition, Ramana suggests self-enquiry. When the mind arises as a thought, do not follow it and further fragment that natural happiness. Enquire, 'For whom is this thought? Who am I?'. Such a devotee is Ananya Bhakt, says Sri Krishna. Out of all devotees - one seeking distress removal (*Aarthi*), one seeking true knowledge (*Jijnasu*), one seeking wealth (*Artharthi*), and one seeking and resting in the Self of all (*Jnani*), the one seeking the Self is called Ananya Bhakt. The inner happiness of such a one is full and complete in itself.

Dr. MK: Happiness is and always will be man's greatest goal. In happiness, one finds the mind relaxed and in a peaceful state. But if one is disturbed, sad, or agitated, the mind is confused and not stable. One should distinguish between pleasure and happiness. Pleasure is sensory and temporary. But happiness is a state of mind. You train the mind to be happy always.

If the mind is clouded by past thoughts and worries about the future, it is always in a state of turbulence. So, in such a disturbed state, one will always find issues and things – even minute silly things – to be unhappy. A child is always happy because it does not have any thoughts to cloud its mind. It looks at its fingers and is smiling happily; it looks at its mother and giggles happily. It lives in the present and hence happiness is permanent.

5.   *"When we are down to nothing, God is up to something "*
NNK: This is a quote taken from the Bible. Psychologists and neuro-biologists thought for many years that learning in living beings took place only in the waking state. Only in the last two decades has there been a study of deep sleep or non-rem sleep. What is surprising is that there is learning in deep sleep. Not only that, there is incredibly better learning.

When the ego does not know, the brain is taught by life itself. The rat that ran around a maze for many hours, exploring many dead-ends before finally finding the food, goes directly to the food the next day. What was learned over several hours is condensed into a package of a few minutes. No wonder we have all been taught to read the Gita or the Bible before going to sleep.

When asked about their source of creativity, Stephen Hawking and Carl Sagan join many great scientists and thinkers in saying 'I do not know'. Many of them agree having got the breakthrough in their sleep. What is meditation but going to the state 'I do not know'. What is surrender except going to that space 'I do not know'. What is misery but a state of 'I do not know' that I don't accept?

When the ego is still, something greater than the ego, the power behind all beings runs our lives. To live a life out of 'I do not know' is a life of creativity and happiness. How to directly go to 'I do not know'? Whenever a thought arises to the ego, do not follow it. Enquire, 'For whom is this thought? Who am I? The 'I' is stilled. When the impulses pushing the 'I' are erased, one goes beyond the ego. Limitless creativity. Limitless love. Limitless awareness. When you are down to nothing, God is up to something. Nay, when you are down to nothing, God alone IS.

Dr. MK: This is the ultimate truth. In the Bhagavad Gita, Sri Krishna talks about total surrender. In verse 66 of chapter 18…

sarva-dharmān parityajya mām ekaṁ śharaṇaṁ vraja

ahaṁ tvāṁ sarva-pāpebhyo mokṣhayiṣhyāmi mā śhuchaḥ

"Abandon all varieties of dharmas and simply surrender unto Me alone. I shall liberate you from all sinful reactions; do not fear."

The stress is on the word *"maam ekam"* – Me alone. There is no one else. If you feel upset, dejected, defeated, and have nowhere else to go and no one else to turn to, I am there. I am the only one you should come to. It is an assertion from Sri Krishna.

All along, Sri Krishna had been asking Arjuna to do two things simultaneously—engage his mind in devotion, and engage his body in fulfilling his material duty as a warrior. He thus wanted Arjun not to give up his **Kshatriya dharma**, but to do devotion alongside it. This is the principle of **karm yog**. Now, Sri Krishna completely reverses this teaching by saying that there is no need to fulfill even material *dharma!!*.

Arjuna can renounce all material duties and simply surrender to God. This is the principle of **karm sanyās**. Here, one may question that if we give up all our material *dharmas* will we not incur sin? Sri Krishna tells Arjuna not to fear; he will absolve him from all sins, and liberate him from material existence.

To comprehend this instruction of Sri Krishna, we need to understand the term *dharma*. It comes from the root word **dhṛi,** which means "responsibilities, duties, thoughts, and actions that are appropriate for us." There are actually two kinds of **dharma**—material **dharma** and spiritual **dharma**. These two kinds of **dharma** are based upon two different understandings of the "self." When we identify ourselves as the body, then our **dharma** is determined following our bodily designations, obligations, duties, and norms. Hence, serving the bodily parents, and fulfilling the responsibilities to society, nation, etc. are all bodily **dharma.** This is also called **apara dharma** or material **dharma.**

6.   ***"Beginning today, treat everyone you meet as if they were going to be dead by midnight. Extend to them all the care, kindness, and understanding you can muster, and do it with no thought of any reward. Your life will never be the same again."***

NNK: This quote is from the American author Og (Augustine) Mandino. His philosophy was that each individual is a miracle and capable of finding success through the universal laws of abundance. As a thirty-year-old, he was on the verge of suicide, when books on self-help uplifted him to a successful career in sales and motivational speaking. He is suggesting an idea to find a new light of discovery from within.

If we treat each person we meet as if he will die by midnight and give them all the care, kindness, and understanding we can muster without expecting a reward, we will discover a new light about ourselves from within. Steve Jobs suggests that we live each day as though we are going to die at midnight. This brings new light about ourselves from within. One expands to new horizons when one serves thus.

In self-enquiry, one erases the individuality of others and oneself and goes for identity with the limitless light of consciousness-existence within. Each time one enquires, 'Who am I?', one removes a bit of the darkness of ignorance caused by individuality and brings in a bit of the light of the limitless consciousness till the ego is completely effaced. Self-enquiry opens new horizons automatically.

Dr. MK: Every life that is born has to die. Death is inevitable. In the Bhagavad Gita, Chapter 2, verse 27, it says

> *jātasya hi dhruvo mṛityur dhruvaṁ janma mṛitasya cha*
> *tasmād aparihārye 'rthe na tvaṁ śhochitum arhasi*

Death is certain for one who has been born, and rebirth is inevitable for one who has died. Therefore, you should not lament over the inevitable.

In the Mahabharata, there is a famous story of *"Yakshaprasna"*, where the four younger Pandavas die without answering the questions of the Yaksha (Yamraj himself) and Yudhishtir answers the 60 questions posed by Yaksha. One of the questions he asked was *"Kim Aascharyam?"* meaning 'What is the most surprising thing in this world?'.

Yudhishtir replies, *"ahany ahani bhūtāni gachchhantīha yamālayam*
śheṣhāḥ sthiratvam ichchhanti kimāśhcharyamataḥ param"

"At every moment people are dying. Those who are alive are witnessing this phenomenon, and yet they do not think that one day they will also have to die. What can be more astonishing than this?" If one understands this, then there is no reason for anyone to treat others without kindness and understanding.

7. *"True wisdom comes to each of us when we realize how little we understand about life, ourselves, and the world around us."*

NNK: These words of wisdom are from Socrates. His basic understanding of life is encapsulated in the view, "I know that I do not know".

Learning through science, humanities, and art over the two thousand years after Socrates, we find that each bit of knowledge or answer, of life, oneself, and the world, throws up many new questions or areas of ignorance. As man found atoms and thought he had found the fundamental particle of life, out came electrons, protons, and neutrons. These opened many areas of ignorance. When man understood three basic forces in the world, the area of quantum opened many more sub-atomic particles opening new areas of ignorance to add to the existing ones. One looks out to the expanses of the space and comes up with dark matter, black holes, and dark energy which open up extraordinary areas of not-knowing. One looks at history. Suddenly, humanity realises that it was only a point of view of events. A new government comes and is eager to rewrite history from another perspective. One realises that one really doesn't know. Art has opened up new areas of the abstract that the viewer's ability to see from infinite angles is what the artist looks to provoke, rather than say anything particular.

One looks at oneself and agrees with the greatest creative people that one has to remain in 'I do not know' to be really creative.

Moreover, Socrates also asks us to 'Know Yourself'. When we enquire, 'Who am I?', and go beyond thought and ego, one comes to the point, 'I know that I do not know myself'. When one has found and rested in this infinite consciousness, one finds the world and God also to be the same, 'I know that I do not know'. One understands that this is the state in total surrender too. The source of true wisdom and true surrender of the limited ego are found to be the same. 'I know that I do not know'. Stillness. True Silence. One is creative not merely to answer important questions of society or science but also every moment of relative life is 'lived' from total wisdom or total surrender of ego.

Dr. MK: Wisdom is a much-maligned word in our vocabulary. Many of us think being wise is being more educated, having more degrees, etc. But if we sit back and think, we will realize that we know so little about so many things in this world. We are but a speck in this vast Universe – called **Brahmandam** in our Vedas – and we think having college education, we know everything.

The Bhagavad Gita in chapter 2, verse 56 says,

duḥkheṣhv-anudvigna-manāḥ sukheṣhu vigata-spṛihaḥ
vīta-rāga-bhaya-krodhaḥ sthita-dhīr munir uchyate

One whose mind remains undisturbed amidst misery, who does not crave pleasure, and who is free from attachment, fear, and anger, is called a sage of steady wisdom.

In this verse, Shree Krishna describes sages of steady wisdom as: 1) *Vīta rāga*—they give up craving for pleasure, 2) *Vīta bhaya*—they remain free from fear, 3) *Vīta krodha*—they are devoid of anger.

An enlightened person does not allow the mind to harbour the material frailties of lust, anger, greed, envy, etc. Only then can the mind steadily contemplate transcendence and be fixed in the divine. If one permits the mind to brood over miseries, then the contemplation on the divine ceases and the mind is dragged down from the transcendental level. The process of torture works in the same manner. More than the present pain itself, it is the memories of past pain and apprehensions of future pain that torment the mind. But when the mind drops these two and has to simply grope with the present sensation, the pain surprisingly shrinks to a manageable (within the limits of tolerance) size. It is well known that historically Buddhist monks adopted a similar technique for tolerating torture from invading conquerors.

Similarly, if the mind craves external pleasures, it runs to the objects of enjoyment and is again diverted from divine contemplation. So, a sage of steady wisdom does not allow the mind to hanker for pleasure or lament for miseries. Further, such a sage does not permit the mind to succumb to the urges of fear and anger. In this way, the mind becomes situated on the transcendental level.

8. ***"When we quit thinking primarily about ourselves and our own self-preservation, we undergo a truly heroic transformation of consciousness."***

NNK: These words of self-transformation are from Joseph Campbell, well-known for his description of the hero's journey which is not only the journey of mythical and real-life heroes but also the journey taken by every living being. The journey appears as though it is in the outside world. It begins as a naive version of the hero in a 'normal' world who gets a call to adventure by circumstances or destiny. The hero refuses to take up the call and denies the existence of the challenge. However, eventually, he takes it up and finds mentors to guide him in this new unknown world.

Retirement from a job of 35 years could be a call to adventure. There are thresholds to the new world where the hero may fail many times before finding new ways, new friends, and new approaches to tackle the new world. Great crises involving greater dimensions and even threatening the whole world or all humans are faced with courage. Many failures only strengthen the resolve. The crisis is overcome and the hero has learned something that is required by all people of his earlier world. He returns. The return is marked by more challenges as he has to master two worlds - the inner transformation that he wants to share and the norms of the outer world. He succeeds in this endeavour too.

The journey, though appearing to be in the outside world is a journey of inner transformation. Unless one stops thinking of one's status quo and takes on the adventure, this journey of self-transformation is not possible. This journey can also be done inside out. Know yourself in self-enquiry. Go the whole way to the inner core where the ego is slayed. That wisdom of the Self will take care of the 'return' to this world, if necessary. Moreover, abiding in the Self frees one of the feelings that one was in bondage and was liberated. No one is really bound. The necessary words of communication arise and get erased in the Self. Not even that. The Self alone is.

Dr. MK: What a wonderful deep meaningful thought this is. Recently I read a beautiful story by Elizabeth Gilbert. Here it is. "Some years ago, I was stuck on a crosstown bus in New York City during rush hour. Traffic was barely moving. The bus was filled with cold, tired people who were deeply irritated with one another, with the world itself. Two men barked at each other about a shove that might or might not have been intentional. A pregnant woman got on, and nobody offered her a seat. Rage was in the air; no mercy would be found here.

But as the bus approached Seventh Avenue, the driver got on the intercom. 'Folks,' he said, 'I know you have had a rough day and you are frustrated. I can't do anything about the weather or traffic, but here is what I can do. As each one of you gets off the bus, I will reach out my hand to you. As you walk by, drop your troubles into the palm of my hand, okay? Don't take your problems home to your families tonight, just leave them with me. My route goes right by the Hudson River, and when I drive there later, I will open the window and throw your troubles in the water.'

It was as if a spell had lifted. Everyone burst out laughing. Faces gleamed with surprised delight. People who had been pretending for the past hour not to notice each other's existence were suddenly grinning at each other like, is this guy serious?

At the next stop, just as promised, the driver reached out his hand, palm up, and waited. One by one, all the exiting commuters placed their hand just above his and mimed the gesture of dropping something into his palm. Some people laughed as they did this, and some teared up but everyone did it. The driver repeated the same lovely ritual at the next stop, too. And the next. All the way to the river.

We live in a hard world. Sometimes it is extra difficult to be a human being. Sometimes you have a bad day. Sometimes you have a bad day that lasts for several years. You struggle and fail. You lose jobs, money, friends, faith, and love. You witness horrible events unfolding in the news, and you become fearful and withdrawn. There are times when everything seems cloaked in darkness. You long for the light but don't know where to find it.

But what if you are the light? What if you are the very agent of illumination that a dark situation begs for? That's what this bus driver taught me, that anyone can be the light, at any moment. This guy wasn't some big power player. He wasn't a spiritual leader. He wasn't some media-savvy influencer. He was a bus driver, one of society's most invisible workers. But he possessed real power, and he used it beautifully for our benefit.

When life feels especially grim, or when I feel particularly powerless in the face of the world's troubles, I think of this man and ask myself, what can I do, right now, to be the light? Of course, I can't personally end all wars, solve global warming, or transform vexing people into entirely different creatures. I definitely can't control traffic. But I do have some influence on everyone I brush up against, even if we never speak or learn each other's name.

No matter who you are, where you are, or how mundane or tough your situation may seem, I believe you can illuminate your world. In fact, I believe this is the only way the world will ever be illuminated, one bright act of grace at a time, all the way to the river."

A great anecdote that touched me to the core. We carry our burdens for far too long. Let us unwind, throw off our worries and concerns, and start thinking about others, then, we really undergo a phenomenal transformation.

9.　*"Surrender to the flow of the River of Life, yet do not float down the river like a leaf or a log. While neither attempting to resist life nor to hurry it, become the rudder and use your energy to correct your course to avoid the whirlpools and undertow."*

NNK: This art of living inspiration is provided by Jonathan Lockwood Huie, an author of self-awareness books whose vision in life is 'Joyful living for all through conscious choice'.

He begins by allowing for our identity with the individual fighting against the flow of life. The flow of life is from the beginning of time. The flow of life is on many planes. One easily sees the flow of life in the physical area and the plane of the mind. The first inspiration is to go with the flow of life like a leaf or a log. This art not only makes for cooperating with the flow of life but manifests as the habit of not attempting to hurry life or resist it.

Years ago, I was running a 5-kilometre run with the banker friends of a hilly town called Mudigere in Karnataka. The first position was taken by an army jawan working in the security division. When I looked at what he did better, I found that he ran downhill fast and slowed down uphill, conserving energy.

In the flow of life, it is not merely conserving energy but learning to use the current of life. When the rudder is merely adjusted for angle, it can divert the boat from whirlpools and undertow, using the current of water. It is the same with sails. Similarly, when one learns the art of flowing with life, one learns to use the rudder of observation and witnessing to avoid the universal problems of working in groups which are currents in the flow of life. Your country could be on the verge of a world war having developed deep enmity to other ethnic groups. This is a current of life. Just as the individual life gets harmonious only in not resisting or not trying to hurry up the flow of life, the life of groups like family, organisations we work for, state, country, religious or spiritual groups, and similar communities small and large, have energies of resistance and hurrying the flow of life. Here, one learns the art of using the rudder of observation and witnessing to avoid the eddies and whirlpools created by such energies.

Buddhism, of course, shows that a mind learning the art of witnessing without judgement, the flow of life in the present moment, can step out of the river of life and witness its flow from the bank.

Dr. MK: A beautiful thought on how to 'go with the flow'. We have heard many thought leaders and gurus speak about going with the flow, not resisting and being one with nature, etc. But how to go about it is the question. In our daily whirlpool of action-packed lives, do we have the sagacity and patience to 'go with the flow' or 'let go'? It is a tough ask indeed. But can we take some concrete steps in this direction? Definitely yes. First, we should stop overthinking. Overthinking is exhausting. When you overthink, thoughts run circles around your head and you find yourself stuck in reverse, unable to move forward. More so, you start coming up with bizarre ideas that totally contradict each other. You start blaming yourself for things you didn't do and worrying about scenarios that may or may not happen.

Overthinking is simply the act of "thinking about something too much or for too long." So, some of the following steps could certainly help in stopping this overthinking.

Change The Story You Tell Yourself

I always used to say out loud: "I can never be on time. I'm not a morning person. I can't commit to anything." Well, guess what? I was never on time for meetings, I was always grumpy in the mornings and I couldn't commit to anything—a job, a relationship, or a side project. *That's because we are the stories, we tell ourselves.* What you repeatedly say to yourself—and how you repeatedly describe yourself—is what you come to believe and be. Everything we do and experience stems from our identity and underlying set of beliefs. Instead, do this: Identify those limiting beliefs and make a conscious effort to stop yourself whenever you catch yourself voicing them. Immediately replace those negative narratives with positive, empowering thoughts: "I am in charge of my emotions", "I think clearly" and, "I'm a decision-maker."

Let Go of The Past

Overthinkers often ruminate about the past. When they do, they're exerting energy on the "what if" "I wish" and "I should have"... But that energy is removing them from the present moment. The past cannot be changed—but you can change the lessons, meanings, and perspectives you extract from it. When you accept the past for what it was, you relieve yourself from its weight. You will then free your mind from the burdens, mistakes, or grudges of the past that stop you from taking action in the present. Learning to let go of the past is something we must constantly work on because it's so easy to slip back into the habit of rumination. This is essential. as it clears up the mental space that was occupied by overthinking.

Stop Your Thoughts in The Moment and Practice Being Present

In the heat of overthinking, stop and say: *"No. I'm not going to have these thoughts right now. I'm not going to give in."* Bring your attention to where you are - here and now. Being in the present isn't easy. It requires practice. But whenever you notice your mind ruminating about the past or wandering into the future, try to bring it back to this moment and think: "The past doesn't matter. The future is out of my reach. All I have in my control is this present moment. So, I will stop thinking about the past or the future. I will only think about the here and now."

Focus on What You Can Control

Author Amy Morin says: "When you find yourself worrying, take a minute to examine the things you have control over." First, acknowledge what's on your mind. Second, take a step back and broaden your perspective.

Identify Your Fears

Very often, it's the irrational fears that arise in our minds that lead to overthinking. We fear what others might think, we fear making a mistake, and we fear not being good enough to succeed. And living in that fear will tangle us in a well of indecision.

Write Down (or Openly Share) Solutions (Not Problems)

High-performance expert Tony Robbins says: *"Energy flows where attention goes."*
To stop overthinking, you must address the problems at hand. When you feel overwhelmed, take some time to write down all the thoughts in your head, but then shift your attention to the solutions. Learn to manage and regulate your emotions, thoughts, and mind. You can build the mental strength for it. Get your thoughts out of your head so you can raise your awareness of them and observe them. Then shift your attention to the solutions you can create to relieve them.

Make The Decision to Become a Person of Action

There are two ideas at play here: making a decision and taking action. One of the challenges of overthinking is that you get lost in the circus inside your head—which then leads you to indecision. This is the worst place to be. Because, if you get stuck in the same place, spinning around in the carousel of your thoughts, forward movement eludes you. What you need to do is practice making decisions and sticking with them. Point the arrow and release it. And do this for the smallest of decisions.

Manage Your Stress: Move, Unplug, Spend Time in Nature

A study that was published in Psychological Science revealed that the brain becomes both calmer and sharper after a person spends time in a quiet setting close to nature. Other research also concludes that walking in green spaces puts the brain in a meditative state. Even a 5-minute walk in the park can have an immediate calming effect on the mind.

10. *'Whenever you hear or read anything of a spiritual nature that moves you or touches your soul, you are not learning something.... You are remembering what you have always known, it is a gentle awakening"*

NNK: This turning-life-around quote is found making its rounds in social media. It is very evocative as the introspection makes one completely turn inward and live the outer life as though in a temporary tent in the courtyard while the inner life is the home.

We could begin by living a life of thinking that the source of spiritual knowledge lies in the outer world. A book or a great mentor brings new information that moves us. We revere the author or mentor, and rightly too. But as we live those findings, we discover that though we had received the information earlier, we did not understand its implications nor could we live it. As the consciousness within becomes clearer, the spiritual information of the book or great mentor becomes clearer. As the consciousness within gets purer, one can live a spiritually transformed life with less and less effort till spiritual life is effortless. Where was this pure consciousness all along? It was always within each one of us. So, any word that spiritually moves us is an awakening to an existing purer consciousness within us.

Self-enquiry takes one to the undivided consciousness ever-present within each one. That is why self-knowledge or enlightenment is called an awakening rather than a journey where we learn from a book or another wiser one, though it appears so.

Dr. MK: Spiritual awakening means different things to different people. It can happen spontaneously, like all of a sudden you become aware of an unseen, non-physical connection to another dimension and you no longer feel separate and alone in the world.

It can happen gradually, as when you learn something from a spiritual teacher and routinely receive guidance from them so that over time, you slowly wake up to your true nature.

Spiritual awakening is what we call the developmental stage of self-actualization. It can begin early on in life, starting in childhood and gaining momentum when forming our identity during adolescence. Psychologists agree that one needs to have formed an individual identity first, to experience the "self," but full actualization of the self includes identifying with all of humanity, which is an evolutionary developmental stage of humankind as a whole.

If spiritual awakening just happens and there is nothing more to learn and there is no one to teach you how to handle your new state of being, misunderstandings can arise. A spiritual awakening "experience" can be perceived as a symptom of a mental illness. This is why spiritual guidance from a teacher is often recommended when practicing spirituality. Spiritual awakening doesn't "just happen" to everybody. It is more likely to happen to those who have had their developmental needs met, but this is not always the case. An abrupt change in one's life or circumstances that shakes the bedrock of your belief system can give you an alarming jolt that wakes up the spirit and connects the mind-body-psyche complex with the soul.

Often, we "wake up" first and then learn about what our "wake up" experience means later. Without guidance, being "awake" can be frightening, disorienting, and maddening. There are real dangers to be aware of, like your 3rd eye opening and a fragile mind not being able to handle this visual feast of psychic information. How to tone it down, yes? This is why a guru, teacher, or spiritual advisor is suggested for new practitioners.

I have experienced such sudden insights when I used to read Puranas, scriptures, and other spiritual readings. Does it mean that I have awakened all of a sudden?

For example, I have been doing regular ***parayana of Sundara Kandam of Valmiki Ramayana*** for more than 30 years now. But every time I read the slokas, I sometimes get new insights. For instance,

Chapter 32 of Sundara Kandam is titled '***Sita Hanuman Darshanam***'. Now why is it called ***Darshanam*** and not ***Veekshanam***, which is the Sanskrit word for seeing?

Is there some inner meaning to this? I kept on thinking and finally realized that Sita Devi's sighting of Sri Hanuman is an epochal moment in the Ramayana and it indirectly kindles one's mind about the ***Deiveeka Avatar*** of Sri Hanuman here. I have been reading this many many times in the last 3 decades or so, but the sudden insight into this came only one morning! The quote which is given above adds more meaning to me now.

11. ***"Prayer is a State of mind, where an amazing EXCHANGE happens..... We hand over our worries to GOD and He hands over His Blessings to us."***

NNK: These simple words of faith are from Dr. Hishmi Jamil Husain, Head, of Biodiversity and Corporate Sustainability, Tata Steel. These words of faith can also be understood or accepted by the scientists who agree with Tom Chi that 'Everything is connected'. In his video, Tom Chi points out that one could live in the world out of this understanding that everything is connected.

Whenever one asks for something, one is praying to that which connects everything. When this asking is consciously done, we call it a prayer to God. Whenever we pray to God, an amazing exchange does happen. We hand over our worries to God and He hands over his blessings to us. When we understand that everything is connected and consciously live out of this identity, our individual achievements are handed over to that connecting energy. The individual worries are consciously handed over to that connecting energy and one lives in the blessing that one is a manifestation of the cumulative learning of life.

When I take up this task of connecting great thoughts of great thinkers or knowing oneself, I am not working as an individual alone. Though I cannot claim to be aware of all knowledge gained by evolving life, whatever I know is out of that connected existence. The body I have is the collective learning of life from the creation of stars in the Big Bang. The language I use, limited by my understanding, is a learning of connected life for over a hundred thousand years. I am standing on the shoulders of all the great thinkers who ever lived. When I struggle with a connection to be made in the flow of thought, I struggle with the understanding that I am praying to the connecting energy. Whether I get an answer or not, my struggle is immediately handed over and my mind becomes calm from the understanding that I am not the doer.

Self-enquiry, in one sense, is a prayer to the one connecting energy, the source of all thinkers and thought itself. Finding and being at the source, makes one understand that all living beings are praying all the time, whether they know it or not. The amazing exchange happens in each living being in deep sleep where one hands over one's worries and is given temporary rest of mind as a blessing. In self-knowledge, the blessing is unbroken.

Dr. MK: Prayers are always answered. God listens to each and every prayer from the heart. Countless people have experienced the miracles of prayers. Devotees of saints like Swami Sivananda, Kanchi Sankaracharya have experienced countless miracles. The moment they leave their worries and problems in Their Hands, they get resolved miraculously. In every religion, prayer has been given primacy. Because, once you Trust HIM and believe in HIM, then nothing can stop you from getting HIS blessings.

In the Bhagavad Gita, Sri Krishna says this about prayer and worship in chapter 12, verses 6 and 7.

"ye tu sarvani karmani
mayi sannyasya mat-parah
ananyenaiva yogena
mam dhyayanta upasate"
"tesam aham samuddharta
mrityu-samsara-sagarat
bhavami na cirat partha
mayy avesita-cetasam"

"Sri Krishna said: O Arjuna, but those who worship Me, giving up all their activities unto Me and being devoted to Me without deviation, engaged in devotional service and always meditating upon Me, having fixed their minds upon Me, O son of Pritha—for them, I am the swift deliverer from the ocean of birth and death."

12. ***"When we love, we always strive to become better than we are. when we strive to become better than we are, everything around us becomes better too."***

NNK: This meditation on love is by Pauli Coelho author of books like Pilgrimage and The Alchemist. He had a spiritual awakening in the year 1987 on a 500-kilometre walk along with his mentor. This awakening is expressed in the book 'Pilgrimage'. The mentor teaches him meditations on love - agape, philia, and eros. Agape is the love of God for humans and the reciprocal love of humans for God; philial love is in relationships and includes love of oneself; eros is love involving the union of the opposite sexes. He says that at the time of his spiritual awakening, he was doing what he loved in almost all aspects of his life. He was writing, having given up successful work as a lyricist; living with someone he loved; and loving the unexpected trek with a mentor. In this quote, he is going to the root of his findings on life. If you love, you will strive to make yourself better. When you love and lovingly make yourself better constantly, you are a source of love, happiness, and striving for the better in any team you belong to.

Ramana Maharshi points out that there is a supreme love of oneself found in everyone. What is the source of this love for oneself found in everyone? To whom is this meditation on love? Who am I? The source of the I is limitless love. Love alone IS.

Dr. MK: The phrase "when we love, we always strive to become better than we are" by Paulo Coelho suggests that when we truly love someone or something, it motivates us to improve ourselves and strive for personal growth and development. Love can be a powerful force for change and self-improvement, pushing us to be the best versions of ourselves. How can we become better? By being a person that is loving and being loved. It will transform your thought processes into positive ones and you can see the difference you are making to yourself and others surrounding you. That is a real metamorphosis.

When someone becomes better, the world around them becomes better. The light shining from you when you become better, inspires others. The thoughts of others of often changed for the better. If you improve your life, the life of others is improved. If you become better, the world is a better place.

13. ***"Those who flow as life flows know they need no other force."***
NNK: These words on the art of living are from Lao Tzu.

We find Kiran Bedi enter sports and give a breakthrough for Indian women to enter sports and shine. We see Sachin Tendulkar score the first double century in a fifty-over cricket match after a long time of one-day matches of fifty overs for each side having been played. Suddenly, many others follow. We hear from Tom Chi that the iron atom in human blood has been created by the death and regathering of stars for billions of years. We, at least in our bodies, are made of star material. We find a small bacteria work over a billion years taking in carbon dioxide and releasing oxygen to create the ozone layer under which higher forms of life could evolve. I use language which has evolved over a hundred thousand years.

We humans are all connected in the subconscious mind, find psychologists. Carl Jung finds similar Archetypes (good and evil forces of life) in the subconscious across various cultures. Tendulkar is a phenomenon, not an individual. So is each one of us. We are all moving in the way in which life flows. How to flow with the flow? If I know where I have to go, I use my limited knowledge. I am worried about why I am where I am and not somewhere else. When I surrender to the flow of life, I understand and accept where I am; I do not restrict my flow by knowing where I could be. The limited knowledge is used sensitively to learn the Art of Life that is flowing from the beginning of creation.

'Not knowing' is the source of their creativity in science say Stephen Hawking, Carl Sagan, Richard Feinman, and many other scientists. Can't one live so creatively all of life instead of merely for scientific exploration? For whom is this creative, flowing with the flow? Who am I? When I stay with 'not knowing' who I am or limiting myself, I live as Lao Tzu is pointing. One flows with the flow of life and does not need any other force except that flow. When the 'I' is dismantled in the limitless source, the flow of life too is absorbed in the limitless source of Pure Being.

Dr. MK: We have been told to 'go with the flow'. Well, what does it really mean? In the Bhagavad Gita, we have messages that talk about how we should be doing our karma without attaching ourselves to the result.

In Chapter 2, verse 70, it says,

āpūryamāṇam achala-pratiṣhṭhaṁ
samudram āpaḥ praviśhanti yadvat
tadvat kāmā yaṁ praviśhanti sarve
sa śhāntim āpnoti na kāma-kāmī

Just as the ocean remains undisturbed by the incessant flow of waters from rivers merging into it, likewise the sage who is unmoved despite the flow of desirable objects all around him attains peace, and not the person who strives to satisfy desires.

The ocean is unique in its ability to maintain its undisturbed state, despite being inundated by the incessant flow of rivers into it. All the rivers of the world constantly empty themselves into the oceans, which neither overflow nor get depleted. Shri Krishna uses the word **āpūryamāṇaṁ** (filled from all sides) to describe that even the rivers pouring all their water during the rainy season into the ocean cannot make it overflow. Similarly, the realized sage remains quiescent and unmoved in both conditions—while utilizing sense objects for bodily necessities, or being bereft of them. Only such a sage can attain **śhānti,** or true peace.

This is a very apt representation of what the quote says. How to achieve this state? Only by surrendering unto HIM.

14. ***To speak gratitude is courteous and pleasant, to enact gratitude is generous and noble, but to live gratitude is to touch Heaven."***
NNK: This meditation on gratitude or thankfulness is by Joannes A. Gaertner, a well-known professor of art history, and a much-admired poet and theologian.

To say 'thank-you' and generally, all speech made with an underlying thankfulness is most courteous to the listener or listeners and surely pleasant on the ear. To enact thankfulness is generous and noble.

An action emanating out of thankfulness to life for what it has given so abundantly and unasked will be an act of similar nature, abundantly giving, unasked. Such a one is sensitive to the needs of the co-traveler and is generous and noble without being asked, and without the receiver feeling low about the act of receiving.

But, for the very breath, thought and spirit of one to be imbued with the single energy of thankfulness or gratitude is to bring heaven to this place 'here' and at this very moment 'now'. The ego sinking into the limitless, abundant, ever-loving, ever-present source allows one to be thankful without pride. The fragrance of liberating gratitude is always present in such a one.

Dr. MK: Living in gratitude is a practice that masters have shown. In the Bhagavad Gita in chapter 3 verse 12, Bhagavan Sri Krishna says to Arjuna that unless you live in gratitude you cannot sacrifice your desire or ego, in that moment not align with the Universe or demigods. For, He says that they cannot be SATISFIED. We are much stuck to the words so we go on doing things with our desire to satisfy the Universe or demigods. In the process, we find only frustration and we find that we are cheating ourselves. Just live Enthusiastically and see how you will be in Gratitude. In that Gratitude, you will be a Giver and not a Receiver. Receivers always have a lot of expectation and desire. They are greedy and seek to steal. Don't follow the words but live Enthusiastically and you will find that you can live this verse in your actions.

It is said in the Bhagavad Gita, '*Yadrccha-labha-santusto Dvandvatito Vimatsarah.*' Whatever is coming to you, you should have some level of contentment, and with contentment comes gratitude. If you are discontent, how can you be grateful? If you are grumbling, you can't be grateful, and if you are not grateful, how can there be grace? Just stop complaining! Know that this whole life is like a dream. It is all going to end and everything is going to finish one day. This very awareness will bring a shift in you. 'This story is going to end someday and the curtains are going to fall' Suddenly, knowing this a shift happens from running to having more contentment. It will come to that.

15. *"The Ordainer controls the fate of souls in accordance with their past deeds. Whatever is destined not to happen will not happen, try how hard you may. Whatever is destined to happen*

will happen, do what you may to stop it. This is certain. Hence, the best course is to remain silent".

NNK: This spiritual insight is from Sri Ramana Maharshi. As a boy of seventeen, having undergone the death experience or enlightenment experience in his Madurai home, he comes to Tiruvannamalai without informing his mother. About two years later, she comes in search of him to Tiruvannamalai having got information about his living in Tiruvannamalai as a boy-monk. She tries to call him back and fails. To console her, he writes out this message on a slate. To the believers, this has remained a great solace and instruction in the practice of devotion and surrender to the one power of the Ordainer.

On the face of it, this statement appears totally fatalistic and gives no free will at all. But it posits that one can learn to be silent in all circumstances. All circumstances, including where the relative existence is completely wiped out, can be crossed by the practice of absolute surrender. The absolutely surrendered will is totally free and in control.

From the perspective of Jnana or absolute awareness, the relative world of actions and results has no real existence. So, the question of whether something will happen or not, cannot arise there. In self-enquiry, one lets go of thought and enquires 'Who am I?'. In one sense, this is the surrender of thought (actions and results) and ego (self-surrender or ***atma-samarpanam***) to the Ordainer. The Ordainer is reached as the power of the absolutely self-attentive thought energy. When this Ordainer energy is held without asking for anything, that too quietens down into completely effortless being-awareness-bliss.

Dr. MK: Lord Krishna affirms in Bhagavad Gita chapter 2 verse 17 that, it is the consciousness that pervades the whole body and is the basic principle by which a living body differs from the dead body.

> ***avināśi tu tad viddhi***
> ***yena sarvam idaṁ tatam***
> ***vināśam avyayasyāsya***
> ***na kaścit kartum Arati***

Meaning: "That which pervades the entire body you should know to be indestructible. No one is able to destroy that imperishable soul."

In Vedas, the soul is referred to as *jiva or atman*. But in the impure state, the *jiva* is encaged in a physical body. This embodied soul is continuously migrating from one body to another including the present body. Krishna is telling this at the beginning of the Bhagavad Gita because Arjun was lamenting that he has to kill his teacher and his grandfather whom he loved so much. Krishna assures Arjuna: "My dear friend, there is nothing called death, it's simply an illusion." The soul never dies. When death comes, all our subtle desires dissolve in our mind, and that mind carries us to a new body. Just like the air carries the aroma of a flower from one place to the other, the subtle body carries the soul from one body to the other.

16. *"At times our own light goes out and is rekindled by a spark from another person. Each of us has cause to think with deep gratitude of those who have lighted the flame within us"*.

NNK: This is yet another quote from the mystic, Albert Schweitzer. He is, in one sense, expressing his gratitude to the 'being in Christ', which he discovers through his meditations on the path of 'Pauline Mysticism', the finding of one's being in Christ. Christ is that state of consciousness within us where the karmas and punyas and papas; actions with good and bad results of all beings who ever lived in the past or live now or will ever live, is taken on and transcended. He is showing his gratitude to that one person who will take him beyond this temporal plane. In 1997, I met VKLV Kumar who turned my life from total darkness by lighting the spark within me by giving his time and meditations selflessly for more than four years. I have ever afterward retained my gratitude to him.

I, with that light, sparked up and discovered Ramana Maharshi who teaches self-enquiry. He points out that only when I am attached to my 'body', I am trapped in a world of complex karma extending over time and place. When I detach inwardly from my physical body, the point of 'being in Christ' is reached.

When enquiry continues beyond personalities, all divine personalities arise after the rise of the 'I' thought. When self-enquiry continues, it takes one to that self-luminous self beyond all personalities, time, place, actions, merits, and sins. My gratitude to

Kumar, Ramana, and other deities I have worshipped, including my family deity Murugan, gets absorbed into that one light of the Self-luminous Self.

Dr. MK: We have all had people in our lives who rekindled a spark in us. Our lives and our work, require much of us; we don't live lives of isolation but rather live in a culture of teamwork and support. There are times when we fall and need others to help pick us up. There are times we have the amazing opportunity to rekindle the spark in others; the time when we get to pick others up.

In our tough times, we have been nursed, nurtured, mentored, and guided by well-wishers to whom we must ever remain grateful. I have felt that I have to take multiple births to repay those who have helped me in my times of trouble.

Today, take a moment to thank those people in your life who continue to support and partner with you; thank those who rekindle the spark when you felt the stress of the world around you. Make a call, send a text, or personally touch base with someone who keeps you going when times are tough. Let's not limit our thanks for our victories and successes . . . let's give thanks to those in our lives who bless us and make us who we are today.

17. ***"You've got to dance like there's nobody watching, Love like you'll never be hurt, Sing like there's nobody listening, And live like it's heaven on earth."***

NNK: These inspiring words on 'union with supreme happiness through work' are from William W Purkey, writer and educationist.

It is said of the great Carnatic music singer, Smt. M.S.Subbulakshmi, that she would not sing a song on stage unless it was practiced many times in no one's presence, with eyes closed. When the audience is not present, or even when they are, the song is an offering to the whole creation or the Supreme Being. It is important to note that not only the audience is closed out but the singer too should be closed out. The practice of a million times the dance or the song erases the singer and dancer. The body is no longer operated for humans by a human. The ego is not worried or elated as practice has made the performance effortless. This effortlessness is the bliss experienced by some rare performers who have offered themselves and their performance to all life. There is no singer or dancer and pure life alone exists.

When one loves and lives with all one's heart, there is no ego. That egolessness brings bliss in the way one lives with people loved with all one's heart. Such people have the experience of heaven on earth. The speaker, singer, dancer, the artist can all experience this heaven on earth. In self-enquiry, this 'ego' or 'being', separate from others, is directly addressed and erased. Everything done is done egoless. In traditional spirituality, such egoless one is living in a world of freedom from bondage as God's energy flows through him. To experience this egoless living is to realise the omnipotence of the supreme. When such living is natural, such a one is in a liberated dimension from egoistic bondage. Such a one is taught by that egoless living realising grace or omnipotence, that knowing the pure energy beyond individuality is knowing everything, the omniscience of the supreme being. The one who lives in this egoless living of constantly knowing and seeing the supreme spirit everywhere and in everything is taken beyond the acts of knowing and seeing God as a separate being. God alone IS. The Supreme Spirit alone IS. The song, singing, singer, and the world of the audience are absorbed in one spirit.

Dr. MK: This quote is also attributed to Mark Twain. In today's world, it seems more than ever that someone is watching our every move. It could be because we post our lives on social media, opening ourselves up to praise and criticism. It seems rare that we keep moments to ourselves, and yet there is power in the self-reflection that takes place when you engage in movement for you and no one else. So how is it that we are supposed to "dance like no one is watching" when everyone is? How do we embrace this practice when it is our job to perform in front of others? How can we, as dancers and dance educators, apply this principle to our dance performance, career, and life outside of dance?

You might think it requires dancing in the dark where no one can see you or indulging in an alcoholic beverage (if of age) to lower your inhibitions and awareness of others watching you, but I assure you, there is more to it. To me, it means dancing free from judgment, criticism or fear of what others might think. It means being present and not overwhelmed or consumed by others' expectations. It means focusing on why I started dancing in the first place — for fun, for expression, for connection, for me!

In today's world, it seems more than ever that there is someone watching our every move. It could be because we post our lives on social media, opening ourselves up to praise and criticism. It seems rare that we keep moments to ourselves, and yet there is power in the self reflection that takes place when you engage in movement for you and no one else. So how is it that we are supposed to "dance like no one is watching" when everyone is? How do we embrace this practice when it is our job to perform in front of others?

Sing like no one is listening, dance like no one is watching, so that we don't need to care whether others like our performance or not. We do it just because we want to. We shouldn't do things because others ask us to so that we can easily hate them. Only when we are willing to do these things will we put effort into them and become better at them.

If we can be ourselves and follow our heart instead of influencing others, even though we are still on earth, we just live like we are in heaven.

18. ***There are only two ways to live your life. One is as though nothing is a miracle. The other is as though everything is a miracle".***

NNK: This quote on the art of daily living is taken from the words of Albert Einstein.

There is a statement in almost all major religions and spiritual paths that every moment is a tiny miracle created by the Supreme. One can clearly understand that such a one is living a life of constant amazement not measured by mind or logic. When an event happens, preceded and followed by events, the gap between two events is immeasurable, a miracle. To such a one, who does not connect one event or thought with the preceding and succeeding ones, every event, every thought is an amazing miracle.

The other way to live is to see that every event and thought is connected to the preceding and following event and thought. The gap is the connecting energy like the string connecting the beads in a necklace. All happenings are connected and flowing. There is nothing that the individual can do but surrender unconditionally to all happenings. This unconditional surrender too frees one from happenings unconditionally and one lives free and with a constant wow!

In self-enquiry, the ego is erased and one understands both the ways to indicate an egoless being. The unconditional surrender and pure limitless awareness are natural to the egoless being.

Dr. MK: There are only two ways to live your life. One is as though nothing is a miracle. The other is as though everything is a miracle. But without deeper reflection, one knows from daily life that one exists for other people; first of all, for those upon whose smiles and well-being our own happiness is wholly dependent, and then for the many, unknown to us, to whose destinies we are bound by the ties of sympathy.

A hundred times every day I remind myself that my inner and outer life are based on the labour of other people, living and dead, and that I must exert myself to give in the same measure as I have received and am still receiving.

Living as though nothing is a miracle: This perspective suggests perceiving the world through a lens of scepticism and rationality, focusing on the mundane aspects of life. People who adopt this viewpoint may rely solely on empirical evidence and scientific explanations, dismissing any notions of wonder or spirituality.

A person who believes that everything in life can be explained by science and rejects any notion of divine intervention or supernatural occurrences.

A scientist who approaches research with strict adherence to empirical evidence and disregards any subjective experiences or unexplained phenomena.

Living as though everything is a miracle: This perspective encourages embracing a sense of awe, wonder, and gratitude for the world around us. It involves finding beauty, meaning, and significance in even the smallest aspects of life.

A nature enthusiast who sees every flower, bird, or sunset as a magnificent expression of beauty and finds joy in the simplest natural occurrences.

An artist who finds inspiration in the everyday world, viewing every moment as an opportunity for creativity and self-expression.

A human being is part of a whole, called by us the "Universe," a part limited in time and space. He experiences himself, his thoughts and feelings, as something separated from the rest - a kind of optical delusion of his consciousness. This delusion is a kind of prison for us, restricting us to our desires and affection, for a few persons nearest us.

Our task must be to free ourselves from this prison by widening our circles of compassion to embrace all living creatures and the whole of nature in its beauty. Only a life lived for others is worth living.

19. ***"All know that the drop merges into the ocean, but few know that the ocean merges into the drop".***

NNK: This pointer to realising the Supreme is from the verses of saint-poet of the 15th century, Kabir. He held that all living beings have emerged from one light and, therefore, there cannot be real evil. That one light is called by different names in different religions.

Here he is referring to the fact that all understand the individual soul, on death, merging into the ocean of one light from where all come. Some religions believe the drops take birth again and again. However, few know the happening of the ocean merging the droplets. This is called self-realization. When the ego, which feels separate from others, enquires into its source, it drops its identity with body and mind. Such an ego in search of truth, drops all false supports, and it becomes still in self-attention. This complete detachment from all creatures is a space that can be entered into only and only by the pure light of the Supreme. The individual is freed of its 'drop' nature and the sea has entered the droplet. This is self-realisation called ***Para-Bhakti*** (transcendental devotion) in the Bhakti Marg. This effacing or erasing of the drop, allowing the ocean to enter it, by stilling the ego, is the core practice in self-enquiry.

Dr. MK: We all know the famous verse

Om Puurnnam-Adah Puurnnam-Idam Puurnnaat-Purnnam-Udacyate

Puurnnashya Puurnnam-Aadaaya Puurnnam-Eva-Avashissyate ||
Om Shaantih Shaantih Shaantih ||

Meaning: Aum! That is infinite, and this (universe) is infinite. The infinite proceeds from the infinite. (Then) taking the infinitude of the infinite (universe), It remains as the infinite alone. Aum! Peace! Peace! Peace!

The Infinite fits in a drop as well. Ocean is an allegory to the infinite. Drop to infinitesimal. You can shrink and fit the infinite in an infinitesimal is what Kabir is referring to. Science is close behind. The earth for e.g., can fit in a marble in a black hole.

Do you know that sensation of being in a room and feeling the entire atmosphere shift when someone walks in? I suppose we all have different degrees of sensitivity to this, but I'm sure you've had that experience. For me, it's particularly obvious if it's someone I'm close to and they walk in fuming with anger or overcome with sadness. Before they even speak, I can feel a palpable change in the energy of the room. It's as though their energetic wave is crashing on the shore of my own.

When I'm well rested and grounded I maintain my ability to let that wave pass right through me, creating a ripple that returns to stillness, I can stay centred while letting them have their own feelings. When I'm stressed out, overtired, and overworked that wave can make me unsteady or even knock me right off my feet and carry me away.

We all have so much in common. The atoms that make up our body's molecules, and the iron that courses through our veins all have a shared origin in the explosion of stars. We're all connected through biology, shared history, and geography – floating together on this tiny blue marble together. We share many of the values that define our humanity – to have a purpose, to feel fulfilled, to be healthy, to be happy, and to be safe even though we may disagree on the form those values take. We're all born, we all die and we're all connected by the atoms and the molecules that course through us, and through everything, like tiny points of light illuminating our life.

Our thoughts, feelings, and actions have vibrations that send ripples into the world around us. Did you know that the electromagnetic field of your heartbeat can be measured several feet outside of your body with specialized equipment? We're literally sending waves of our presence out around us.

The energy of the people around us can affect our emotions and our strength in a very tangible way. This is why I'm so intent on choosing the people I surround myself thoughtfully. I want a community that helps me laugh more, helps me feel more connected to what's real and most important, and who I can turn to when I need help.

With a supportive community, we can harness power to give us courage, boost our energy reserves, jump higher, or run farther. When we're surrounded by the energy of a group we commit more fully, we engage more deeply, and it increases our own capacity to do whatever it is that we want to do. We're held more accountable for the way that we show up in the world.

Many people feel at a loss to find the time or opportunity to create a community that helps them with their deepest challenges and lifts them to their highest potential. We don't always find that in the communities where we engage the most, like the family we're born into, or in our workplace.

20. ***"Cling to the one who clings to nothing; And so clinging, cease to cling."***

NNK: This simple teaching on realising Truth is by Tiruvalluvar in his work Tirukkural dated anywhere between 500 BCE to 500 CE.

Here, the sage-poet is writing on realising the Truth through renunciation or detachment. According to the sage, there is an energy that is self-reflective, self-luminous, independent of anything and everything. It is this nature of independence from anything and everything that is considered the authentic test for Truth or Supreme Being by spiritual teachers. Truth is free of need of any support. It does not have a cause or an effect outside of it. All relative existence must happen only 'within' this independent, self-luminous consciousness. The teaching contained here is for the relative individual to hold on to that one energy and let go of all other supports. This is the path of Japa (chanting one Name or Mantra) and Dhyana (meditation on that one energy).

By clinging to the one energy that is free from all attachments, one lets go of all other attachments and is finally rid of separate individuality apart from that Truth. In self-enquiry, one begins the spiritual journey with the hypothesis that if Truth is independent of all supports, how can anything exist independent of that Truth? So, I need not seek Truth as something from which I have an independent existence, but take it that my existence is dependent on the Truth. So, when thought arises, I do not cling to it. I let go of thought by enquiring, 'For whom is this thought? Who am I?'. The Truth of the self-attentive, self-luminous Self stands revealed when all clinging is dropped. Ramana Maharshi asks one to hold that energy and be still. That energy too reveals its stillness where self-knowing or self-luminosity is just True Being.

Dr. MK: Renunciation is a common central thought in Indian spirituality and philosophy. What Tiruvalluvar says here is essentially the essence of all Indian spiritual thought. In the Bhagavad Gita Chapter 6, verse 2, Sri Krishna says

yam sannyasam iti prahur yogam tam viddhi pandava
na hyasannyasta-sankalpo yogi bhavati kashchana

What is known as sanyās is non-different from Yog, for none become yogis without renouncing worldly desires.

A *sanyāsī* is one who renounces the pleasures of the mind and senses. But mere renunciation is not the goal, nor is it sufficient to reach the goal. Renunciation means that our running in the wrong direction has stopped. We were searching for happiness in the world, and we understood that there is no happiness in material pleasures, so we stopped running toward the world. But the destination is not reached just by stopping. The destination of the soul is God-realization. The process of going toward God—taking the mind toward Him—is the path of Yog. Those who have incomplete knowledge of the goal of life, look upon renunciation as the highest goal of spirituality. Those who truly understand the goal of life, regard God-realization as the ultimate goal of their spiritual endeavor.

Many persons renounce the world to go and live in monasteries, only to find that in a few years, the renunciation has vanished and the mind is again attached to the world. Their detachment was *phalgu vairāgya*. Finding the world to be troublesome and miserable, they desired to get away from it by taking shelter in a monastery. But when they found spiritual life to be difficult and arduous, they got detached from spirituality as well. Then there are others who establish their loving relationship with God. Motivated by the desire to serve him, they renounce the world to live in a monastery. Their renunciation is **yukt vairāgya**. They usually continue the journey even if they face difficulties.

In the first line of this verse, Shree Krishna states that a real **sanyāsī** (renunciant) is one who is a yogi, i.e. one who is uniting the mind with God in loving service. In the second line, Shree Krishna states that one cannot be a yogi without giving up material desires. If there are material desires in the mind, then it will naturally run toward the world. Since it is the mind that has to be united with God, this is only possible if the mind is free from all material desires. Thus, to be a yogi one has to be a **sanyāsī** from within, and one can only be a **sanyāsī** if one is a yogi.

21. ***"Let the bonds of the world come to an end, The vast universe has opened its arms,***

   The soul is fearless to know the great unknown."

NNK: These words on liberation through expansion of consciousness are from the great Indian poet, Rabindranath Tagore. He is known for his philosophy of asking one to see God in each and every object of the world. From this 'known' God, he is taking one to the unknowable God. The bonds of the world are seen when one sees God in form. There is a connection between forms that allow for birth and death. He asks the reader to open up to the vast universe. Is the cosmos expanding or not? What is the reality of matter? Are black holes in the cosmos or the cosmos in the black holes?

The mind goes beyond the known into the unknown. The mind stops measuring. The mind stops seeing discrete objects and their gaps. The great unknown is not dark but full of the light of surrender. The great unknown is beyond all individuality. The great unknown is the source of all creativity. The great unknown is beyond the bounds of creation and creativity. The great unknown is the omnipresent liberty available to all.

In self-enquiry, the truth of the individual and individuality are directly enquired with the quest 'Who am I?'. The immanent unknown is the transcendent unknown. The duality of knowledge and ignorance is transcended in the being where the immanent unknown is one with the transcendent.

Dr. MK: Rabindranath Tagore's spiritual outlook and humanism were derived from man, nature, and Brahma or God. He held the view that the route to spiritual development was from 'body to society, from society to totality and from totality to the spiritual domain'. In this way, the melody of the soul was intertwined with the universal power. But what was required for this intermingling was connecting the world of nature with that of human beings. To Tagore, the whole human body appeared to be reverberating with the touch of light, air, affection, love, bliss, joy, and electricity, as if embedded in a supernatural flute. Although he might have been influenced by the romantic movements of the time, the Brahma Samaj, the Bauls, Sufism, or the Vedanta philosophy of Upanishads, those views were in some respects Tagore's very own. We can very well comprehend how his spirit was liberated by connecting with the universe, nature, and the environment that surrounded him, by looking at the following lines:

"Where He has given himself up through his infinite mirth and youthfulness, there is no dearth of affluence there, no limit to variety, and the riches are unending. There, the sky is lit in a thousand directions wearing the girdles of stars; there, beauty surfaces in so many new forms, the gushing of the spirit never stops."

By connecting with our environment in this manner, our self-consciousness becomes sweeter, deeper, and brighter. The man within us grows into a fuller entity. Our soul seems to mingle with His colours and flavour. Rabindranath Tagore had identified this phenomenon as devotion. He said, "The poet's task is to ignite this awareness in the consciousness of man, to transform indifference into a newer zeal. That poet is great in the eyes of humans who diffuse human hearts with the attributes of constancy, grandeur, freedom, omnipresence, and depth." This theme of liberation of the spirit is found in many of Rabindranath's poems. There is thus a new excitement for self-expansion in 'Kalpana' "Oh bird, my bird / blind, don't fold your wings now". The formula for revival of the self encompassed the spirit of the universe. This inseparability of the self is made clearer in the poem *'Anobachchhinna Ami'* "I saw under the infinite sky / I rock while seated on the swing of light". In the *'Geetanjali-Geetimalya-Geetali'* phase, the soul of Tagore could become one with the cosmos.

Spiritualism had transcended all aspects of his life and he looked at man and nature as images of God. He wrote in a letter, "If I have realized God or got any hint about him, then it was from this world, its people, trees, animals, dust and soil from all these objects." We, therefore, find the poet comprehending God as dearest to man and his companion in times of sorrow, as in the volumes of *'Geetanjali'-'Geetimalya'-'Geetali'*. In *'Balaka'* (1916), he depicted God as the determinant of human destiny. Ultimately, this God finds His place in the heart of man and becomes one and the same in the eyes of the poet.

22. ***"God is in all and in the seer. Where else can God be seen? He cannot be found outside. He should be felt within. To see the objects, the mind is necessary. To conceive God in them is a mental operation. But that is not real. The consciousness within, purged of the mind, is felt as God."***

NNK: This statement bridging Bhakti (devotion) and Jnana (awareness) or God as unconditional love and God as unconditioned consciousness is from Ramana Maharshi.

So far as one is identified with a form, there is always worship of God with form. Even though one may not worship with tradition, the reverential God images, one worships so many objects. Each object desired is God at that moment. One worships or seeks objects for the contentment of the mind and gets disappointed as the mind itself is unreal.

The outward-turned consciousness of the mind is present in waking and dreaming and gets inward-turned involuntarily, and unconsciously in deep sleep. Once rested, the mind is pushed outward on waking, towards its pet objects and away from objects of aversion. To see another, the mind is required and that mind is unreal - present in waking and dream but vanishing in sleep. To imagine God in each one is a mental operation. It is posited that unconditional love is to see God in all. Though it is felt that by seeing God in everyone, the mind will be quiet and contented, it will not be quiet once it thinks of another.

So, the mind purged of all thoughts will be the consciousness that is in self-attention, self-luminous. Such consciousness purged of thoughts is felt as God. Worship of form is impossible to avoid when one is identified with body-mind. Worship of form is impossible for the one who has erased the ego. Worship of form will gradually purify the mind and bring it to self-awareness. Unconditional Love and Unconditioned Consciousness are one as the Self.

Dr. MK: In The Bhagavad Gita, Sri Krishna says that He is God. He claims that there is nothing superior to Him. He claims that He is the source of all spiritual and material worlds, He claims that everything emanates from Him. He claims that He is the seed-giving father of all who take birth in the material world and that material nature is working under His direction. He claims that He is time.

He claims that no being - moving or non-moving - can exist without Him. He claims that He pervades the entire universe in His unmanifest form. He claims that He is the basis of the Brahman. He claims that He has always existed and always will. He claims His body is transcendental and never deteriorates. He claims that fools cannot understand His transcendental nature as the Supreme Lord of all that be.

Shri Krishna claims to know everything that has happened in the past, all that is happening in the present, and all things that are yet to come. He also knows all living entities, but Him no one knows. Everything is within Him and He is within everything, but still, He exists independently from the creation because He is the source of the creation. He says He can only be seen directly by undivided devotional service.

He says He is the taste of water, the light of the sun and the moon, the syllable Om in the Vedic mantras; the sound in ether, and ability in man. He says He is the original fragrance of the earth, and the heat in fire. He is the life of all that lives, and the penances of all ascetics. He is the original seed of all existences, the intelligence of the intelligent, and the prowess of all powerful men. He is the strength of the strong, devoid of passion and desire. So, God is there in everything and everyone. In the Hindu customs, we pray to each and every living being as a manifestation of the Bhagawan.

23. ***"We know that the train carries all loads, so after getting on it why should we carry our small luggage on our head to our discomfort, instead of putting it down in the train and feeling at ease?"***

NNK: This pointer about surrender is from Ramana Maharshi.

Self-attention, when silent naturally, is beyond all powers. But, when it raises as 'I-I', it is the radiant power of the Self. This power is the Ishwara Shakti worshipped in many religions under many names. Ramana points out that just as in the presence of the Sun, all actions go on in this world, just so, in the presence of the radiance of the self-attentive power, all actions go on in all planes of existence. This power of presence has no want or aversion. It is called as unaffected witness. It is this power of presence that gives **karma phala** without itself being affected. It is this power that Ramana calls existence- consciousness shining as 'I-I'.

When this power of presence is the one power running all creation, why should the ego feel it is carrying its load? Understanding this, one can let go of thoughts in self-enquiry. If the thought of daughter, son, father, or mother arises in self-enquiry, surrender to that one power taking care of everything, allows us to let go of that thought. The practice of surrender is not only helping in self-enquiry, but it can also by itself erase the ego and merge into the power of the presence, the power of 'I-I', the Self.

Dr. MK: Bhagavad Gita keeps talking about detachment and how you should be doing your karma and not worry about the result. That is attachment with detachment. If you keep doing your duty and still keep on carrying the burdens on your head, then where is the surrender? And where is detachment?

The first step towards detachment is to realise that we are the masters of our emotions, our desires, and all our attachments. Detachment is not about having no emotions or desires, but having control over our emotions, actions, and desires and being able to manage them. Free our emotions of love from the sense of control, and we are free of our emotions! Free our actions from the worry of their results, and we are free of actions! Have as many desires as we want, but have the wisdom to know which desires we want to follow and the ones we do not want to, then we will be free of desires.

Letting go is an art that we need to practice and develop. Letting go is the way to detachment. Detachment is about having freedom. It is beautifully described in the following lines, "Like Buddha before us, letting go is gaining freedom. Once we let go of trying to control everything, life seems to flow with greater ease. It's not unlike a twig floating down a meandering river. It doesn't't try to stop or force the current into an unrealistic upstream reversal of flow. It just lets go and enjoys the ride. Letting it take it where it will."

Chapter 18 of the Gita summarizes all about letting go; Lord Krishna says, "Let go, do not cling on to the fruits of your actions. Have no attachments to the result of your actions (do not worry about what is going to happen). Perform your prescribed duty as shunning away from the responsibilities that come with your birth is not renunciation, but an illusion due to your ignorance."

24. ***"When one door closes another door opens; but we so often look so long and so regretfully upon the closed door, that we do not see the ones which open for us."***

NNK: This quote from antiquity present in all cultures is also attributed to Alexander Graham Bell and Helen Keller.

When we lose a wonderful job or reach the age of superannuation or retirement, we spend all the time worrying about what is over. The lost job or the position and identity lost, keep bringing depression to us.

The whole world of opportunities is now open to us. Righty looked at, we now have the opportunity to look at so many doors that are open and take a call on which one we like. The Bhakta who has surrendered his personal worries with faith, feels frustrated that this faith is unable to do anything about the fault in a friend. I keep feeling that my faith has closed its doors. But, when, instead of finding fault with the friend, I genuinely worry about him, I now have made that my personal worry. Now, my faith expands to cover the worry about my family and friends. I see the faults of others and realise that all I have to do is to make it my worry, by being compassionate and not merely fault-finding. My faith now envelops all. It is here that Sri Krishna says in Chapter 10 that he who has faith in God and has enveloped all in that faith and trust is given Buddhi Yoga. Here the Jeeva can do no further. He can remain still in faith and intellect. Sri Krishna assures that when the door of human effort ends, the door of limitless light opens. That limitless light removes our ignorance completely and opens the door of Self - Realisation. Don't worry about one closed door. Many are open. Choose the one you want to enter and keep going. There are no closed doors or open doors. There is only light.

Dr. MK: Most people are too attached to the past, to what they are familiar with, and therefore, miss opportunities that stand right in front of them.

Doors may close, but there are always, other, unlimited number of doors – new opportunities. The world is full of opportunities, if we could only see them. The Infinite Power is boundless, and so the possibilities are without number.

Not every plan works out. Sometimes, there are losses and failures. Sometimes, there are problems in relationships. Sometimes, people lose their money or job or meet other unpleasant things. We don't always have control over these events, but we can exercise control over our minds and attitudes.

When one of these events happens, and we focus our attention on the loss – the closed door, we see only a closed door with the resultant frustration and unhappiness.

If we could only move our sight and attention away from the closed door, we might be surprised to discover new, open doors. It might not be so easy to move our eyes elsewhere, due to attachment to the old and familiar, and fear of the new and the unknown.

If you find it difficult to stop the stream of uncontrolled negative thoughts, your mind will keep focusing on the loss, failure, and frustration – on the door that has closed. Would these thoughts help you in any way, or will they create suffering, and prevent change and improvement?

How can you free yourself from past attachments and see the new opportunities? How can you bring yourself to see, and enter the new doors that open for you?

To enter, you need to make some effort: by being aware of your thoughts, developing self-discipline, controlling your mind, and trying for inner peace. All these will help.

Mindfulness/Witness

1. ***"The key to growth is the introduction of higher dimensions of consciousness into our awareness."***

NNK: This is a teaching of Lao Tzu a great saint of Taoism. When I read aloud as a part of my learning my ninth standard Geography, I am using my larynx or sensory body. The mind may or may not be focused. When I start learning without making sound, the mind has less opportunity to wander. I do a Pooja at home by chanting Vishnu Sahasra Nama. My mind goes wandering at the tenth Name of Vishnu and suddenly realises its wandering and rejoins the muscle memory of the larynx in the 100th Name or so. I realise that meditating on God's Name with mind attending to mind is better Pooja.

When I listen to another with that attention, my day is full of Pooja. My listening is disturbed by judgement when I listen with like and dislike. I start listening without liking or disliking. The consciousness within frees itself from the world of sight, sound, touch, fragrance, and taste. It looks at its own thoughts without likes and dislikes. The consciousness frees itself from the mind. For whom is this thought of witnessing thought without like and dislike? Who am I? The triad of witness, witnessing, and witnessed gets absorbed in the self-attentive Self. The limited ego which separates oneself from others and limited happiness are merged in the Source.

Dr. MK: What is consciousness? A question that immediately comes to my mind when I see this quote. Nandu has beautifully explained the connection with mind, body, and intellect – the Sat, Chit, and Anand. In the Bhagavad Gita in chapter 2, verse 17, Sri Krishna says,

avināśi tu tad viddhi
yena sarvam idaṁ tatam
vināśam avyayasyāsya
na kaścit kartum Arati

That which pervades the entire body you should know to be indestructible. No one is able to destroy that imperishable soul.

This is consciousness, which pervades the entire body. It is further said in the Bhagavad Gita that this consciousness is immutable, immovable, un-burnt, un-cut, un-wet and always existing (eternal), but we don't see such traits anywhere in the physical realm. Our experience says anything can be burnt in no time. This is an experience that is beyond our current experience of physical space and time. Consciousness is a divine experience. When situated in consciousness, one becomes freed from ignorance and is situated in knowledge and transcendental joy.

2. ***"We are shaped by our thoughts; we become what we think. When the mind is pure, joy follows like a shadow that never leaves."***

NNK: When we are in a positive frame of mind, all things we do and people whom we relate to get enveloped in that positive thought energy. When we are angry, jealous, or in a sense of shame, what we do, or the people we relate with, get enveloped by this negative thought energy. So, that we are shaped by our thoughts seems to be a fact difficult to set aside.

But then, the Buddha, who uttered these words also mentions the 'pure mind'. So, in Buddhist thought, one has a thinking mind which is enslaved to shaping itself by thought and there is an 'observing' mind that can observe that 'I feel my depression', 'I feel my anger', and 'I feel my shame'. Such a mind has detached a bit from its slavery to thought.

However, purity comes only when such observation is free of like and dislike. Then one sees the dropping off of anger, hatred, jealousy, and even the positivity that could be thrust on others, leading to enslaving oneself. When the witnessing mind frees itself of all thoughts both positive and negative, it is said to be in a state of mindfulness or purity in the present moment, moment by moment.

'For whom is this thought? Who am I?', is called self-enquiry. Here consciousness frees itself of even witnessing and identifies with the Self of all. Sri Krishna calls such a student of life as 'Ananya

Bhakt' - one who doesn't see anything other than the Self of all. The universal witness, called Mindfulness by Buddhism, ensures the Yoga and Kshema of such a practitioner of Ananya Bhakti. Yoga is finding union with the Supreme. Kshema is protecting that Union as unbroken. It is also taken that the worldly needs of such a one are carried by the Unaffected Witness, the Ishwara. To such a one with a pure mind that transcends slavery to thought, happiness is but natural.

Dr. MK: A beautiful and invaluable thought indeed. In the Advaita philosophy, there is a ***Jeevatma and Paramatma***. There is a saying that goes like this – In a tree, there are two birds, one is eating the fruit and the other is observing it. What deep meaning The Gurus have given to these! The observing bird is the Paramatma and the eating bird is ***Jeevatma. Jeevatma*** is the ***Abhasa Rupam of Paramatma***. This is exactly what is discussed above. The thinking mind and observing mind are not different and not the same either. You have to detach yourself from the other one.

Barbara O'Brien (2019) further expands on this by explaining the word ***'vijnana'***, which means awareness or consciousness. In one context, ***vijnana*** is the thing that connects an organ and an outside object to create a mental experience, e.g., it connects the eye and an object to create the experience of 'seeing'. If we analyse the issue, we will see that the objects of the world and we who confront them are nothing more than a series of experiences mediated by ***vijnana***, in our minds. In order to realise the third aspect of Yogacara, 'the perfected aspect', we must realise that this flow of experiences that our mind wrongly separates into subjects and objects is all that reality is, and the only reality we can know.

O'Brien also writes that Yogacara added two more 'consciousnesses', really meaning sensory organs, to the six already taught by early Buddhism, with the second of them being ***'alayavijnana'***, known as 'storehouse consciousnesses'. This is where the 'seeds' of our past karmic actions are stored, to later come to the surface either in this life or another. She says there is some similarity between this Yogacara doctrine and Sigmund Freud's later psychoanalytic idea of the unconscious mind which stores our experiences, ideas, or memories that are too powerful or painful to consciously process but will affect us until we face them head-on.

3. *"How far you go in life depends on you being tender with the young, compassionate with the aged, sympathetic with the striving, and tolerant of the weak and the strong. Because someday in life you will have been all of these."*

NNK: George Washington Carver is taking up the Golden Rule of Ethics in his own way. The golden rule commonly found in all religions and spiritual paths is, in one way, put as, 'Do unto others as you would have them do unto you'.

When I was young, the tender care of my mother and some teachers allowed me to not crumble from timidity which seemed to envelop me. Even the youth of today, not so timid, but bristling with resistance to authority needs tenderness from us. The old mother-in-law who had given over 30 years to taking care of our household needs compassion now when she remembers nothing other than her work routine. That she stares like a deer blinded by headlights when we lose compassion and become irritated, must be observed with care and healing brought by compassion.

When I was striving to achieve in life, I found a true friend in VKLV. Kumar who was sympathetic to my efforts but firm when I wanted to cross ethical limits. He was tolerant of me when I felt weak and depressed and tolerant when I felt unduly optimistic. I understand, what Carver means.

To carry out the golden rule of doing unto others as I would have them do unto me, I cannot afford to be blinded by my impulses. Impulsive living prevents living by any rule of life, let alone the Golden Rule of ethics. When impulses arise as thought, I let it go and enquire, 'Who am I?', to whom this impulse arises. Only when the 'I' is freed of all impulses, can it really carry out the Golden Rule. If one is in bondage, how to be tender to the young, compassionate to the aged, sympathetic to the striving, and tolerant of the weak and strong? Self-knowledge is at the root of ethical life.

Dr. MK: The "Golden Rule" was proclaimed as the second commandment by Jesus. Many commentators, speakers, and Gurus have spoken on similar lines, expanding the thought through their own wisdom. In the Bhagavad Gita, we see Karma being discussed in detail. In the last chapter, chapter 18, verse 23 says..

niyataṁ saṅga-rahitam arāga-dveṣhataḥ kṛitam

aphala-prepsunā karma yat tat sāttvikam uchyate

"Action that is in accordance with the scriptures, free from attachment and aversion, and done without desire for rewards, is in the mode of goodness."

In the Mahabharata, regarding proper action, it says,

ātmanaḥ pratikūlāni pareśhāṁ na samācharet

śhrutiḥ smṛitiḥ sadāchāraḥ svasya cha priyamātmanaḥ.

"If you do not like it when others behave with you in a certain way, then do not behave with them in that way either. But always verify that your behaviour is in accordance with the scriptures." Conduct yourself with others as you desire them to behave with you.

4. ***"More often than not, anger is actually an indication of weakness rather than of strength"***

NNK: This great thought is from the Dalai Lama (XIV). The words are so framed that there seems to be some exception, but generally speaking, anger is an indication of weakness rather than of strength. What could be the exception? Mahaperiyava, Sri. Chandrashekarendra Saraswati, the pontiff of Sankara Mutt, Kanchipuram points out an exception. When recounting those people whom he respected, apart from his mother and Guru among others he mentions a girl who is angry with her younger brother in the streets of a town in India. The pontiff says that she resorted to anger as the younger brother had erred and she wanted him to uplift himself. So, anger as an instrument of a person for the welfare of a careless individual is not a weakness.

Other than these situations when anger is used as an instrument of compassion, one is under the sway of anger. One is enslaved by anger. Such anger destroys relationships built over decades, breaks down social structures, and dismembers the good persona built over many years. Such anger is indeed a weakness. For whom is the anger? Who am I? Free the 'I' from all anger and let the 'I' merge in its source. Let there not even be an intent to use anger to uplift. That source is the unity of all life. It can only uplift. When Ramana sees that people have brought down thousands of leaves of a mango tree while bringing down mangoes carelessly by hitting the branches with a stick, he is said to have roared in anger at those who injured the tree.

Dr. MK: Man is a compendium of emotions. Many gurus and thought leaders have talked about negative emotions and feelings like anger, hatred, revenge, resentment, etc., and how these thoughts totally reduce and destroy a person. Of all the negative emotions, anger is the most dangerous one. It consumes a person completely and can lead to rash and irresponsible actions too.

In the Bhagavad Gita chapter 2, verse 63, it says,

krodhād bhavati sammohaḥ sammohāt smṛiti-vibhramaḥ

smṛiti-bhranśhād buddhi-nāśho buddhi-nāśhāt praṇaśhyati

"Anger leads to clouding of judgment, which results in bewilderment of memory. When memory is bewildered, the intellect gets destroyed; and when the intellect is destroyed, one is ruined."

In anger, people commit mistakes that they later regret, because the intellect gets clouded by the haze of emotions. People say, "He is twenty years older than me. Why did I speak in this manner to him? What happened to me?" What happened was that the faculty of judgment was affected by anger, and hence the mistake of scolding an elder was made. When the intellect is clouded, it leads to bewilderment of memory. The person then forgets what is right and what is wrong, and flows along with the surge of emotions. The descent continues from there, and bewilderment of memory results in the destruction of the intellect. And since the intellect is the internal guide, when it gets destroyed, one is ruined. In this manner, the path of descent from divinity to impiety has been described as beginning with contemplation of the sense objects to the destruction of the intellect.

This reminds of a popular story. A man and woman had been married for more than 60 years. They had shared everything. They had talked about everything.

They had kept no secrets from each other except that the little Old woman had a shoe box in the top of her closet that she had cautioned her husband never to open or ask her about. For all of these years, he had never thought about the box, but One day the little old woman got very sick and the doctor said She would not recover.

In trying to sort out their affairs, the little old man took Down the shoe box and took it to his wife's bedside. She agreed that it was time that he should know what was In the box. When he opened it, he found two knitted dolls and a stack of money totaling $95,000.

He asked her about the contents.

'When we were to be married,' she said, 'my grandmother told me the secret of a happy marriage was to never argue. She told me that If I ever got angry with you, I should just keep quiet and knit a doll.'

The little old man was so moved; he had to fight back tears. Only two precious dolls were in the box. She had only been angry with him two Times in all those years of living and loving. He almost burst with Happiness. 'Honey,' he said, 'that explains the dolls, but what about all of this money? Where did it come from?'

'Oh,' she said, 'that's the money I made from selling the dolls.'

THE DAY YOU LEARN TO CHANNELISE YOUR ANGER, YOU CAN GET WHATEVER YOU WANT!

5.   *"Never let the future disturb you. You will meet it, if you have to, with the same weapons of reason which today arm you against the present.".*

NNK: These words of Marcus Aurelius, the Roman emperor who was also a Stoic philosopher, indicate that the reason within oneself can transcend circumstances and time.

For this reason, he meditates while leading a war campaign. He meditates that reason should not wait for circumstances to be tranquil. The reason should be independent of service from others. The reason should not be pushed into action by passion. When one learns to deal with the present with such reason, one understands that the future is nothing but living out of this tranquil, transcending reason. The future is nothing but moment by moment living in the present with a reason that is not pushed by impulses. Such a one is not disturbed by the future or even the present.

The impulses that threaten reason are accumulated as the ego. To live in pure, tranquil reason beyond time, one has to dismantle the ego.

Whenever an impulse rises as a thought, do not follow it. Enquire, 'For whom is this thought? Who am I?'. Keep erasing the impulses till the ego is completely dismantled.

Dr. MK: Living in the present is advice given by many. Bhagawan Sri Sathya Sai Baba says, *"Past is past. The future is uncertain. The present is not an ordinary present; it is the 'omni' present.*

On many occasions, Baba has talked about living in the present. He says, "We either think of the past or the future and ruin the present. Past is past, forget it. The past which is dead and gone, is useless. Work for your progress by living in the present, and in the moment. The future does not always bring happiness. And, so far as the past is concerned, how much happiness have you experienced in it? Therefore, live happily in the present. What should we do in the present? Follow this maxim: Less luggage more comfort makes travel a pleasure. We should not worry about the past at all. Thinking about the past will not do any good to us. Therefore, we should lead our life in the present and achieve all-round progress."

Eckhart Tolle, A German-born spiritual teacher has written many books. And, in one of his books, The Power of Now – A Guide to Spiritual Enlightenment, says, "In the normal, mind-identified or unenlightened state of consciousness, the power and creative potential that lie concealed in the Now are completely obscured by psychological time. You cannot find yourself by going into the past. You can find yourself by coming into the present. Life is now. There was never a time when your life was not now, nor will there ever be."

Sri Sri Ravishankar, the spiritual guru, says, "Live in the present moment. The present moment is inevitable". Living in the Now and not worrying about the Future is the only way to be at peace with oneself.

6. ***"There are monks, unborn, unbecome, unmade, unfabricated. If there were not that unborn, unbecome, unmade, unfabricated, there would not be the case that escapes from the born, become, made, fabricated would be discerned. But precisely because there is an unborn, unbecome, unmade, unfabricated, escape from the born, become, made, fabricated is discerned."***

NNK: These are the words of the Buddha.

This quote points out directly to enlightenment and that which is beyond creation here and now. As Sri Krishna points out in the Gita, whatever is born has to die. We find the Stoic Marcus Aurelius meditates on death every moment to be free of attachment to created beings and thus get enlightened. That which is born has to face the opposite - death.

What has become something is bound to unbecome. We become an engineer by waking and having a lucid brain and losing it in sleep or when the brain loses data. Anything made will be unmade. Anything fabricated or put together will be dismantled.

The ego is at the root of all birth, becoming, making, and fabrication. It is dismantled in self-enquiry. Whenever a thought arises or is born, one should not follow it. One should enquire, 'For whom is this thought born? Who am I?'. The ego is dismantled thought by thought, part by part. Even time and space are put together only after the ego arises. When the ego is dismantled, the unborn, uncreated, unmade, unfabricated reveals itself. Buddha is pointing out that since this unborn, uncreated, unbecome, unfabricated exists, there is liberation from the created, the area of becoming, the field of bondage.

Dr. MK: Buddha talks about this in Nibbana Sutta. Nibbana is nothing but the same as Nirvana in Hindu scriptures. How to attain the state of Nirvana is explained in many of the scriptures.

Nirvana or "nibbana" as it is popularly called, is the final extinguishing of all desires and bonds and mental modifications arising from them. It is resting in total and unconditional peace. In a spiritual sense, it is liberation from the evils of impermanence, change, samsara, and the dissolution of the transmigrating individual ego. It is a condition where nothing actually happens, moves, changes, or becomes. It is a state of bliss.

The concept of nirvana means the attainment of an individual's natural state, beyond good and evil. According to tradition, the liberated person does not act or trigger any kind of action, for they work for humanity's sake without moral obligation. Those who achieve nirvana join God and merge their atman (pure self) in perfect communion with divine life. In this state, there is no ego or desire, and the atman is free from any kind of earthly manifestation, for it is one with eternal peace and perfection, also known as the state of yoga.

In the Gita, Sri Krishna tells Arjuna to do his duty. Since he belongs to the warrior's caste, he must lead in war, and by doing so, he will fulfill his dharma. Sri Krishna suggests to him the three disciplines (yoga) of knowledge, devotion, and action. Jnana-Yoga, the discipline of knowledge, instructs one on the magical value of knowledge, through which one knows how to get rid of the consequences of one's actions, and erase all deeds acted out with selfish motives.

Moreover, Bhakti Yoga, the discipline of devotion, proposes the total worship of God. Bhakti culminates with the merging of one's soul with God. That will lead to salvation or Nirvana. The turning point comes with Karma-yoga, the discipline of action, that centers around not expecting any fruits from service. An action's fruits are what causes the samsara cycle to happen, and the solution doesn't lie in the action per se, but in the intentions of the one performing it. Therefore, to free oneself from karma (and achieve Nirvana), one must renounce any kama (desire). In this case, to act will merely mean to conform to one's own ***sva-dharma***, which determines each caste's role within society.

7. ***"So often we are so focused on the finish line that we fail to enjoy the journey".***

NNK: These words are from Dieter F Uchtdorf a German aviator, airline executive, and religious leader. He has pointed to a spiritual fact in typical aviator's words.

Living in the present is a spiritual practice suggested by many schools of meditation. Though Truth has to be omnipresent is one of the tenets assumed by almost all spiritual paths, in which of the three divisions of time can it be searched for and experienced by the individual? The past cannot be acted upon. It is gone. The future has not come. We live and experience life in the Present. So, it is in the present that we would find True happiness or True awareness.

Life is a journey; how do we live? So often, we are driven by goals. What will happen? What will the world say? Will I be remembered? Will my coffee come out tasty? In the present moment alone can find true happiness.

In the present too, there is an object, act of perception, and perceiver. Object and perception are goals. The perceiver alone is ever-present. True happiness can only be found in the ever-present perceiver. For whom is this thought? Who am I?

Dr. MK: Living in the present.. is it possible? Can we forget our past and not worry about our future? Yes, it's possible to live in the moment. You can do this by not allowing yourself to be controlled by thoughts. In meditation, you practice watching your thoughts pass by. You can choose not to attach to the thoughts in your head so you can live in the moment. Getting into a flow state allows you to experience something to the point of losing track of time. You become immersed in something you're passionate about. Doing things you enjoy, meditating, and having fun are all ways to live in the moment naturally. And not worrying about the result or benefit. Leave everything in God's Hands and He will take care of all. Your job is to just keep doing what you are supposed to do.

The Bhagavad Gita talks about attachment with detachment. In Chapter 2 verse 47 is the famous Sloka

karmaṇy-evādhikāras te mā phaleṣhu kadāchana

mā karma-phala-hetur bhūr mā te saṅgo 'stvakarmaṇi

You have a right to perform your prescribed duties, but you are not entitled to the fruits of your actions. Never consider yourself to be the cause of the results of your activities, nor be attached to inaction. Significantly, the Gita recommends detachment, not irresponsibility. That it doesn't condone irresponsibility is evident from the context – after hearing the Gita, Arjuna fought the Kurukshetra war diligently. During the war, he met his forces every morning and evening: morning to finalize the day's strategy; and evening to review that day's battle and plan the next day's strategy. All this planning and reviewing indicates that he was concerned about the results.

Then what does the Gita call for detachment mean? It means that we do not let our consciousness stay caught at the material level, wherein we become elated on getting the results or dejected on not getting them. Thus, Gita's call for detachment from results is meant to free our consciousness from disempowering attachments to material things so that we can become attached to the supreme spiritual being who is far bigger than the results.

8. ***"A mind committed to compassion is like an overflowing reservoir - a constant source of energy, determination, and kindness. This is like a seed; when cultivated, gives rise to many other good qualities, such as forgiveness, tolerance, inner strength, and the confidence to overcome fear and insecurity."***

NNK: Compassion is empathy towards the sorrow of others. In all spiritual teachings, compassion is emphasised. First, it is proposed as a healer. If you don't have proper shoes, feel for the one without a leg. But, the Dalai Lama, who is the source of this kindness-evoking quote, wants us to be committed to compassion.

In traditional Hinduism, this teaching means, to live a life meditating always on compassion. Initially, we may begin with economically lesser-endowed human beings. But then we find many old people, sick people and physically challenged along with those afflicted by mental ailments. Our compassion widens.

We find that even physically, mentally, and economically endowed people are unhappy in relationships. We also widen our compassion to include animals and plants. We meditate further. We find that any living being feeling separate from others is suffering. Now, when we understand that all living beings are suffering, our compassion widens to include inconsiderate, cruel, and downright criminal-minded people. No living being is outside the ambit of compassion.

One sees that 'non-living' substances are also made of atoms and are present inside living beings. Life or consciousness expands to envelop the 'living' and the 'non-living'. The compassion widens to include the whole of creation. For whom is this thought that I am a separate entity? Who am I? Taking the separative ego to the source, one finds the fountainhead of all compassion. There is only one life. No division. The very existence of such a one is brimming with the bliss of compassion towards all.

Dr. MK: Our scriptures and *itihasas* talk about compassion all the time. In Ramayana, Maa Sita talks about compassion. When Hanuman comes and tells her that Ravana is dead, she is extremely happy. Hanuman asks her permission to wipe out the ***rakshasis*** who had given Maa Sita trouble during her captivity by Ravana. Mother Sita exhibited her unlimited compassion and magnanimity when She said that those ***raksasis*** were simply and helplessly working under the instructions of the evil Ravana as his servants and it was not right to punish them. At that time, she told the following story.

Once a hunter in the forest tripped and fell while hunting a lion and lost his weapons.

The lion then started chasing the hunter. The hunter ran and he climbed upon a tree. On the tree, he could see that a bear was sitting. The man was completely helpless and he took shelter from the bear requesting the bear to spare his life. Meanwhile, the lion came to the bottom of the tree and instigated the bear to push the man down so that they could both eat the man. The bear refused saying that the man had taken shelter of him and hence he would not push him down.

After some time, the bear started sleeping and the lion told the hunter, I am feeling very hungry. So, you push the sleeping bear down from the tree so that I can kill and eat him and you can be relieved. The ungrateful hunter, so much concerned about his own life, pushed the sleeping bear. The bear somehow woke up while falling down caught hold of a branch of the tree and was saved. The lion told the bear that even though the bear tried to save the hunter, he was so ungrateful as to push him down. Hence the bear should now help the lion by pushing the hunter. The saintly bear replied that great souls never have an inimical attitude towards others and it is their nature to be compassionate even if the others are of a bad nature. Thus, the bear stood by its principles and did not harm the hunter who was greatly ashamed seeing the behaviour of the bear.

In the Srimad Bhagavatam, we find that saintly Vidura gave good counsel to his brother Dhritarashtra and asked him to get rid of Duryodhana, the source of all trouble.

Hearing this, Duryodhana insulted Vidura very badly calling him a spy, infidel and he desired that Vidura be immediately put out of the palace. Thus, being pierced by arrows through his ears and afflicted to the core of his heart, Vidura quit his brother's palace and went on a pilgrimage.

Dhritarashtra could not speak anything against his son. It is unimaginable for any other person who has been subjected to such an insult to come back and do good for such a brother. But we find that Mahatma Vidura came back after having already adopted the renounced order of life, just for one purpose and that is to deliver his elder brother.

Srimad Bhagavatam 1.13.14 says,

kancit kaalam athaavaatsit sat-krto devavat sukham

bhraatur jyesthasya sreyas-krt sarvesaam sukham aavahan

Thus Mahatma Vidura, being treated just like a godly person by his kinsmen, remained there for a certain period just to rectify the mentality of his eldest brother and in this way bring happiness to all the others.

Such is the compassion of the great souls for all the conditioned living entities who have turned their faces away from Krishna. It is what the compassionate spiritual master does for all of us.

9. ***"Anger and hatred are the materials from which hell is made. A mind without anger is cool, fresh, and sane."***

NNK: This mindfulness quote is from Thich Nhat Hanh who was a Vietnamese Buddhist monk, peace activist, author, poet, and teacher. Martin Luther King Jr nominated him for the Nobel Peace Prize in 1967.

I begin by feeling that heaven and hell are out there. I try to get lots of things and wealth. I try to gather together with people I like. Then, I realise that it is the 'like' within me that creates heaven and the dislike within me that creates hell. When I have negative emotions like anger, hatred, jealousy, and shame, I am in hell. When I have positive emotions like kindness, compassion, love, and peace, I am in heaven.

Do I have control over positive and negative emotions? The findings of Buddhist teachers is that we are not. They suggest that with each out-breath, we identify with the emotions we are possessed by. With each in-breath, we find emotions within us. Let us take anger. When angry, if you are outward turned, you are angry. When angry, if your breath is inward, you have a chance to observe anger. When angry, normally, one is outward turned in the breath. So, to observe the breath is the first step to free oneself from hell.

Positive emotions too are fleeting and the heaven they provide is transitory. Observe your breath and free yourself from slavery to heaven and hell, teaches Thich Nhat Hanh.

Breath and emotions arise after thoughts arise. All other thoughts arise after the 'I' thought arises. Free yourself from negative and positive emotions at the root. Heaven and hell are transcended in self-attention.

Dr. MK: Man is a bundle of emotions and feelings. There are positive and negative emotions and we all know anger, jealousy, hatred, etc. are negative emotions. In fact, anger is one such emotion, that leads to other negative ones. Ancient wisdom says that one who controls his anger can win any battle.

In the Bhagavad Gita, in Chapter 12, verse 13, Gita talks about hatred. Swami Sivananda while giving his commentary on Srimad Bhagavad Gita talks about this verse thus

"He who hates no creature, who is friendly and compassionate to all, who is free from attachment and egoism, balanced in pleasure and pain, and forgiving."

In Chapter 16 verse 21, Sri Krishna says, "There are three gateways leading to hell - lust, anger and greed. One must give these up, for they lead to the degradation of the soul". Sri Krishna, in His dialogue with Arjuna, has analysed the working of anger. When asked as to what impels the man to commit sin, as if by force, even against his own will ; Krishna replied that the root cause of the problem was lust (excessive desire), which when unsatisfied, emerged as anger.

It is the all-devouring and most sinful enemy of mankind (shlokas 3.36 and 3.37). Lust has been called a constant enemy of the wise, because like fire, it has an insatiable appetite (shloka 3.39). It cannot be satisfied for long. It envelops wisdom, and gives rise to frustration and anger. This concept has further been elaborated in shloka 2.62 wherein it has been stated that thinking about sense objects produces attachment towards them. Attachment breeds desire, and non-fulfilment of desire leads to anger. So, we see both anger and hatred – both being negative emotions lead to disruption of peace of mind.

10. ***"The mindful heart is like a garden, full of flowers and trees and birds.***

    It is a place of peace and beauty, where the soul can rest and grow.

    The mindful heart is like a river, always flowing, always changing.

    It is a place of movement and growth, where the soul can learn and evolve.

    The mindful heart is like a fire, always burning, always bright.

    It is a place of passion and love, where the soul can find its true purpose.

    The mindful heart is like a mirror, always reflecting the truth.

    It is a place of self-awareness, where the soul can see itself clearly.

    The mindful heart is a gift, and it is one that we should all cherish.

    For when we have a mindful heart, we can live a more peaceful, more loving, and more fulfilling life."

NNK: Before the year 2003, my view of the world was through thought energy that divided itself as good and evil; right and wrong. It helped me greatly in choosing right over wrong. From 1997, I had the excellent company of my friend VKLV Kumar who was my guide and mentor in re-establishing the holding of right action. That had built my penance. In March 2003, I was introduced to mindfulness meditation. That day was the cricket match between India and Pakistan. I was asked to be mindful in the present moment about the good and bad; right and wrong in me. Before that, I would have great joy whenever things went in favour of India and greatly depressed when Pakistan took the upper hand. That day, I took to mindfulness like fish to water. My eyes were on the Television screen, but my attention, in the present moment, was on the rise of good and bad in me. The joy and sorrow were never outside! I had been superimposing them on the world! From that day, my seeing and listening of the world were attempted through this constant 'unaffected witness'. Thoughts too were directly observed without right and wrong. They dropped away as the consciousness looking at them was detaching itself, freeing itself. Within a year of practice, my resting identity was almost always, the thought-free state.

The practice period is analysed in this detailed poem on mindfulness.

The mindful heart is indeed like a garden full of flowers and trees and birds. It is a place of peace and beauty. The soul can rest and grow in this garden. When I practiced 'mindful hearing', though one was aware of the motives of the speakers, one did not dwell on them. The listening which was undivided (as in hearing good and bad) was free of judgement and rested in the peace of being the unaffected witness.

The soul could learn and evolve.

The soul could find the true purpose of life, being one with the unaffected witness.

The soul could look at itself as the pull and push from others was crossed.

In my case, I still would claim that 'I was thought-free'. It was then that Self Enquiry entered. For whom is the thought-free state? Who am I? This erased the ego and, along with it, the final separation between the undivided, ever-present consciousness and the ego.

DR. MK: This is a beautiful poem by Rumi, that has resonated as deeply in me as in Nandakumar. What wonderful but simple thoughts he has brought out. But is it easy to be mindful? Nandakumar has had a transformational experience guided by a Guru. But for ordinary people like you and I, is it possible to be mindful?

The fact is that we are always clouded with I, me, and mine thoughts. There are some steps you can take in this direction that help you be mindful.

- Let go of the past.
- Accept the present moment.
- Meditate – it really helps but needs to be properly guided by a Guru
- Get in touch with your senses.
- Practice mindfulness in daily routines – like brushing your teeth, pressing your clothes, or simply walking.

Mindfulness trains your brain to be more efficient, focused, and less distracted. It has also been shown to lower blood pressure, improve memory, lessen depression and anxiety, and is associated with increased athletic performance.

Working mindfully is a feeling of being totally in the moment. There is joy, ease, and lightness in your work. Whether you are working at the office, spending time with your family, or in a workout, strive to live in the moment by practicing mindfulness.

11. ***"Life is a balance of holding and letting go."***
NNK: This great pilgrimage of life captured in words is from Rumi, the great poet of the 13th Century. To understand this pointer, we can take a look at another of his poems.

"I died to the mineral state and became a plant,

I died to the vegetal state and reached animality,

I died to the animal state and became a man,

Then what should I fear? I have never become less from dying.

At the next charge (forward) I will die to human nature,

So that I may lift up (my) head and wings (and soar) among the angels,

And I must (also) jump from the river of (the state of) the angel,

Everything perishes except His Face,

Once again, I will become sacrificed from (the state of) the angel,

I will become that which cannot come into the imagination,

Then I will become non-existent; non-existence says to me (in tones) like an organ,

Truly, to Him is our return."

Though one may or may not agree with this evolution of consciousness suggested by the poet, one understands why life and understanding require a balance between holding and letting go. To get a state one has to hold. To stabilise in that state, one should hold. When one sees the limits of a state, one should be able to let go. When one sees the glimmer of new life, one should let go or die to the old and hold the new, evolved way of life. Without dying, life stagnates.

One can also look at the whole journey. Both holding and letting go are thoughts. For whom is the holding and letting go? Who am I? The whole process stands revealed. Only after the I thought is born do the thoughts of old, states to be let go of and new ones to be held arise. Take the 'I' to the source. One exists even in the non-existence of objects, holding, letting go, balance, and the ego. Existence beyond the duality of holding and letting go.

Dr. MK: We have been told – 'don't hold on to material irrelevant things, let go'. But what is the meaning of letting go? Can we let everything go? If not what all should we be holding on to? A question many seekers have sought answers for and answered in their own way. Sri Ramana Maharishi asked the question "Who am I?" and He started the process of *'Atma Vicharam'* or self-enquiry.

Throughout our lives, we are faced with decisions - big and small - about when to hold onto something or someone and when to let go. These choice points can range from numbingly painful to pretty easy. The conscious choice about whether to hold on or whether to let go requires an energetic shift from one pattern of being to another and requires more of us than may be obvious on the surface.

Holding on and letting go is actually about creating a transition. Transition is the process of going from the place that you have been, to the place that you are going (even if you don't know where that destination is). Most of us would prefer a straight shot from one place to the other but invariably there is the dreaded MIDDLE. The MIDDLE is where all of the real action takes place and where your transformation happens.

The first decision is - Do I hold onto what I have or am I ready to let it go? Often the universe decides for you – you lose a job, someone passes away, your partner walks out. In those cases, your situation is immediately torn from you on a physical level. Energetically, you are still very much holding on. There are other times when you actually choose to let go of a situation or person. The fallacy is that is harder when life happens to you but in reality, it is often harder to make the choice yourself. This process of transition (big and small) is one we each go through many times in our lives. To navigate this process well means taking apart what was and putting together what will be. It is not simply holding on or letting go – it is about changing who you are as you do it.

12. ***"The wind carries away the fallen leaves, and the snow melts into the stream.***

   Everything is in a constant state of change, and yet we cling to our illusions.

   Let go of your fears and your desires, and find peace in the present moment.

   Embrace the uncertainty of life, and discover the beauty in impermanence."

NNK: This quote is one of the ways of meditating on impermanence or transience or change that is present in the world. This meditation is at the heart of almost all spiritual traditions.

Science shows that our body exchanges atoms with the earth through food, water, and respiration and exchanges almost 7 percent of body weight every day. In two weeks, over 90 percent of the earlier body atoms are replaced by new ones. Yet we cling to the idea 'I am this body'. The body keeps changing from childhood to youth and from youth to middle and old age. Yet we cling to the thought 'I am the body'. When everything in the world, including one's own body is seen to be subject to constant change, one understands that if one doesn't understand change but wants to cling to something, there will be fear and desire.

One who does not accept change will be afraid of losing what one has and will desire something fixed to give peace. So, to live with change and transience, one has to let go of fears and desires and live with the flow of life in the present moment. When one does not cling to fears and desires one sees the world like a cinema show that does not affect the witnessing consciousness. That is the beauty of peace when everything is seen as a show passing before oneself with constant change but consciousness frees itself as a witness. The witness and the show merge in the undivided, uncreated, unborn source of all.

Dr. MK: Our need for physical security is perhaps an outward gesture of our inner fear of uncertainty. When we finally step into the discomfort—stare at fear face-on—we come out lighter and less fearfully attached.

In turn, we reveal more of who we are at the core: confident, expansive, and totally adventurous. If you're feeling muddled by uncertainty and fear, these ideas may help you navigate these feelings with courage:

Re-think thinking too much. Many of us are conditioned to "think things out." A bombardment of non-stop thoughts rarely gets us anywhere. Honest clarity lies in letting things go, stepping back, and holding space for the unknown. Being present with patience and allowing time to pass is a healing process. Thinking too much and worrying about things that are not in our control has created a worrisome status for man.

Practice acceptance. Befriend not knowing and let go of the need to know what's next. Ease and peace will follow. Resistance and fighting are extremely rigid and draining. Acceptance is fluid, light, and ever-changing. Shifting to an acceptance mindset allows us to show-up, wholly, with our attention grounded in the present, and experience heightened levels of awareness and wisdom. The five 'a' s - adopt, adapt, accept, adjust, and acclimatize - are very critical in attenuating our psychological makeup towards peace.

Remember what's there. Each of us is capable of experiencing an unlimited amount of goodness. When feeling anxious or worried, remember to shed off the heaviness of resistance to reveal what is always underneath: love and freedom. Being good is not tough at all. If you decide to be good, then nothing can stop you.

Understand uncertainty. Our journey will always be laced with hurt, risks, laughter, and celebration. We don't get to cherry-pick only the parts of our path we want to experience. It's an all-inclusive ride. Learning to acknowledge that there will always be uncertainty will allow our experiences to be more meaningful and joyful, regardless of what we may be dealing with.

Find adventure. Think back to an exhilarating, defining, or even life-changing moment. You might notice this memory occurred when you were going with the flow, having faith—even when you couldn't see the big picture at the time.

13. ***"Peace is within oneself, to be found in the same place as agitation and suffering. It is not found in a forest or on a hilltop, nor is it given by a teacher. Where you experience suffering, you can also find freedom from suffering. Trying to run away from suffering is actually to run toward it."***

NNK: This finding by a Buddhist Monk, Ajahn Chah, who belonged to the forest tradition involving meditating in tiger-infested forests and caves, opens up the real place where meditation happens - within oneself.

Meditation which calms the mind and brings peace is not to be searched for in forests, solitary places, or even by great teachers. It has to take place within oneself where ignorance has resulted in agitation and suffering. Observing the agitation and suffering without liking or disliking is Buddhist meditation. When suffering and agitation are witnessed and looked at, without like or dislike, the mind starts quietening towards peace. If one experiences suffering and can detach oneself by observing without like and dislike, one can free oneself of suffering too.

However, instead of facing and observing the suffering within, if one tries to run away into escapes like alcohol or drugs, eating compulsively, in aimless entertainment and other means, one increases the suffering.

For whom is this thought that one is a failure in life? For whom is this shame at having made a terrible mess? For whom is this suffering? When the sufferer is erased, can suffering remain?

Dr. MK: Where do we find peace? A question that every agitated human being keeps asking. And without peace one cannot have a life. In the Gita, Sri Krishna says, 'Know God, know peace'. And a person who cannot control his mind can never find peace. In chapter 2, verse 66, Sri Krishna says..

nāsti buddhir-ayuktasya na chāyuktasya bhāvanā
na chābhāvayataḥ śhāntir aśhāntasya kutaḥ sukham

But an undisciplined person, who has not controlled the mind and senses, can neither have a resolute intellect nor steady contemplation on God. For one who never unites the mind with God there is no peace; and how can one who lacks peace be happy?

Swami Muktananda explains this attachment with a beautiful story. He relates a bee's story. The bee was sitting on a lotus flower, drinking its nectar. As the sun began setting, the petals of the flower began shutting. But the bee was so attached to enjoying the object of its senses that it refused to fly off. It thought, "There is still time for the flower to close. Let me suck some more nectar while I can." In the same way, we can see old age coming as a sure sign of death, but like the bee, we remain engrossed in enjoying worldly pleasures.

In the meantime, it became dark and the lotus flower closed, trapping the bee. It thought, "Never mind! Let me remain inside my beloved flower for tonight. Tomorrow morning, when its petals open again, I will fly away."

Kāṣhṭha bhedo nipuṇopi sangṛihī kuṇṭhito bhavati padma vibhede

"A bee has the power to cut through wood. But look at the attachment to the sense objects, that, the bee which can cut through wood, is stuck inside the soft petals of the lotus." In the meantime, an elephant came, broke the lotus from the stem, and swallowed it. The bee along with the lotus went into the stomach of the elephant. The bee was thinking, "My beloved lotus is going somewhere, and I am happily going along with it." It died shortly thereafter.

Similarly, we humans too remain engrossed in the gratification of the senses and do not heed the message of the saints to engage in devotion to God. Finally, time overtakes us in the form of death. Here, Shri Krishna says that those who refuse to discipline the senses and engage in devotion continue to be rocked by the three-fold miseries of Maya. Material desires are like an itching eczema, and the more we indulge in them, the worse they become. How can we be truly happy in this state of material indulgence?

14. *One is never afraid of the unknown; one is afraid of the known coming to an end."*

NNK: This meditation on the art of living is by Jiddu Krishnamurthy. It is agreed by great thinkers like Stephen Hawking, Carl Sagan, and Richard Feinman on the lines of Socrates that the source of creativity cannot be known by the individual ego. This entering the unknown for a creative answer, is extended by Krishnamurthy to all of life and living.

When one of his long-standing followers is on his deathbed, Krishnamurthy visits the dying man. The follower asks Krishnamurthy to explain death and that whatever is said will be accepted with humility. Krishnamurthy points out that death is unknown and why should one try to bring it to the known. All 'known' is subject to non-existence. The ego and all things 'known' are subject to birth and death.

The ego, which knows, is afraid to let go of the 'known'. It is not afraid of the unknown but merely afraid to end the known. Once it learns the art of letting go or dying to the 'known', it learns about 'not knowing oneself' as a limited entity. It is set unconditionally free.

In self-enquiry, the 'known' that arises as thought is not pursued. One enquires, 'For whom is this thought? (For me) Who am I?' This repeated light of enquiry on the ego erases all the known and reveals the Self beyond the known, the body-mind. Freedom from the 'known' is not something to be afraid of. It is freedom from the cycle of birth and death faced by the 'known' ego.

Dr. MK: Is it possible for the mind to empty itself totally of fear? Fear of any kind breeds illusion; it makes the mind dull, and shallow. Where there is fear there is obviously no freedom, and without freedom there is no love at all. Most of us have some form of fear; fear of darkness, fear of public opinion, fear of snakes, fear of physical pain, fear of old age, fear of death. We have literally dozens of fears. And is it possible to be completely free of fear?

We can see what fear does to each one of us. It makes one tell lies; it corrupts one in various ways; it makes the mind empty, and shallow. There are dark corners in the mind which can never be investigated and exposed as long as one is afraid. Physical self-protection, the instinctive urge to keep away from the venomous snake, to draw back from the precipice, to avoid falling under the tramcar, and so on, is sane, normal, and healthy.

When we seek fulfillment in any form, whether through painting, through music, through relationships, or what you will, there is always fear. So, what is important is to be aware of this whole process of oneself, to observe, to learn about it, and not ask how to get rid of fear.

When you merely want to get rid of fear, you will find ways and means of escaping from it, and so there can never be freedom from fear.

How can you let go? By surrendering to HIM and letting go of all worries and fears. Implicit surrender and belief that HE will take care of us, will enable us to live without any fear.

15. ***"The true value of a human being is determined primarily by the measure and the sense in which he has attained liberation from the self."***

NNK: This great thought of spiritual essence is from the great scientist, Albert Einstein.

He opines that a scientist should not leave spiritual thinking to others and merely depend on those authorities. He independently arrives at the fact that our individuality is an optical illusion. He studies the self or ego as having evolved in time. If the animals had been the originators of the separate ego and then man built on it, all thoughts that were ever thought have gone into the forming of the ego because each thought must have been for a thinker. That thinker has evolved by experiencing all thoughts that ever existed. When all thoughts that ever existed go into the making of the self, to take a few and claim that those few thoughts put together are 'me' is an optical illusion.

He says that this optical illusion can be overcome and reality approached only by expanding one's consciousness. That is possible only by extending an unconditional love towards all others. In other words, the true value of a human being lies only in the extent to which he has erased his individuality and merged in the Self underlying all creation. In self-enquiry, this optical illusion is directly addressed and erased.

Dr. MK: Ancient texts like the Bhagavad Gita, Upanishads, and the Vedas suggest that there are two major paths to understanding one's inner self. The first path is self-assessment, a powerful tool for self-discovery and introspection of one's true nature. In ancient times, meditation was a form of self-assessment. The second path is through our relationship with our surroundings—people, beings, and things.

It is not an easy task to focus on the inner self as our day-to-day life is too distracting. Besides, the natural tendency is not easily acknowledging our weaknesses, and correcting them. Along with acknowledging weaknesses, refining our strengths is also a rigorous task.

Why is it so important to understand the inner self? To be an impactful person, one must first understand who they are, their personality traits, and their true nature. After realisation of one's inner self, utilising one's strengths and values to overcome challenges in life.

In Chapter 7 verse 12 of the Bhagavad Gita, Shri Krishna speaks of three fundamental kinds of human characteristics that is, Sattvic, Rajasic, and Tamasic. Who shall we look up to for Liberation? We usually look for external objects to find our liberation. We say that only if we did not have this or that confinement, we would be liberated. We think that if we had more power, freedom, or money, we would be liberated.

Shri Krishna says that the Brahma, the supreme consciousness is what people should look up to. According to Shri Krishna, true liberation is not attainable by looking into externalities or external objects. The unification of **Atma** (self) with the **Brahma** (supreme consciousness) is the ultimate liberation for an individual.

16. ***"Wisdom does not come from reading books; it is being conscious about the reality of life. When you know that everything is temporary & changing, your mind becomes clear."***

NNK: These words on the art of living are from the founder of the Art of Living Foundation, Sri Sri Ravishankar. According to him, science and spirituality are linked and compatible, both springing from the urge to know. The question, "Who am I?" leads to spirituality; the question, "What is this?" leads to science. Emphasizing that joy is only available in the present moment, his stated vision is to create a world free of stress and violence.

Here, he is pointing to the source of wisdom. The modern intellect, as a flip side to the wonderful learning offered by books, may mistake mere book learning to be wisdom. Books do open the reader to the minds of great thinkers who might have lived even millennia before. But, unless one learns from the actual application of those great thoughts, one is not wise. One is vulnerable to the changing challenges of life.

What is it that one learns from the application of great ideas one learns from books? It is that everything is temporary and changing. Tremendous failures turn into incredible success and Himalayan successes turn into dust. This too shall pass. A student of meditation tells a master that he had great peace and wonderful meditation that day. The master said that this too shall pass. A few days later, the student reported severe dullness of mind in meditation. The master relieved his mind by pointing out that this too shall pass.

All objective experiences are fleeting and changing. When everything is temporary and changing one cannot do anything about it. One remains still. That is the unchanging foundation that is ever-present. All objective experiences arise after the 'I' thought 'arises'. The root of changes, the ego, is taken to the unchanging foundation, letting go of the ephemeral.

Dr. MK: It can be easy to get caught up in the drama of life. Sometimes, it feels like everything is going wrong and that you have no control over your destiny. You may feel overwhelmed by uncertainty or worry about what's to come. In these moments, it can be useful to have a mantra, a short spiritual or motivational phrase that helps you to take a step back and remember that bad times do not go on forever, that all are fleeting, and difficult moments will pass.

For many people, focusing on the mantra "everything is temporary" enables them to break out of negative thought patterns and face the world with a more positive approach. These are incredibly powerful words.

When you repeat the mantra "everything is temporary", it should remind you that everything in life goes through its own cycle. Nothing lasts forever, so there's no point worrying about what might happen tomorrow or pondering on past mistakes; everything has an expiration date and eventually comes to pass.

"Everything is temporary" means that the people you love are also only here for a limited amount of time, so it's important to cherish them while they're still with you because one day things will change forever. When someone dies, some people believe that their spirit lives on in our memories while others prefer to say goodbye completely and not focus on what used to be but rather look ahead to the future.

Knowing that everything is temporary will help you to live a life of non-attachment, not allowing anything to define you or affect your happiness. Living this way is not always easy, it takes presence and self-awareness. We can do some things to practice non-attachment so that we can learn to enjoy everything life throws at us:

- **Practice non-judgement** - Allow situations to be just that, situations, not reflections on your character or worthiness as a person. Don't beat yourself up over anything because it will only make you feel worse and create more problems for you down the line.

- **Stay present** - Being present in the moment is a great way to practice non-attachment. When you can live in the here and now, it becomes so much easier not to allow your fears about what might happen in the future to influence how you feel right now.

- **Be grateful** - Being thankful for everything that you have can help you value each day as an opportunity rather than something that can bring you stress or anxiety. Remembering all of the wonderful things you already have, instead of worrying about getting more, will improve your quality of life immediately!

- **Accept change when it comes** - Remember that being attached to any one thing means, that if anything were to change or go wrong, then it could be very painful. When things go wrong, accept that it wasn't to be, and try to learn from what happened.

Self-Enquiry/Know Yourself

1. ***"Once you become consciously aware of just how powerful your thoughts are, you will realise everything in your life is exactly how YOU allow it to be"*** ...

NNK: The above meditation on the power of thought is by Melanie Moushigian Koulouris, a mom, a writer, and a wife. Forever a student of life, in her own words.

'Coffee' is a thought. 'I am this body' is a thought. 'Let me go to that place' is a thought. 'Let me not go to that place' is a thought. 'Let me dedicate my life to India' is a thought. 'Good and bad; right and wrong, are thoughts that open the gates to heaven and hell' is a thought. 'Witnessing frees consciousness of right and wrong' is a thought. 'Family is my prime commitment' is a thought. 'Cosmos' is a thought. 'Mind is trapped in the body' is a thought. 'The Cosmos is a thought in the mind' is a thought. 'I am a weakling trapped in human form' is a thought. 'All beings are the Supreme Consciousness experimenting with various forms' is a thought. 'Whenever a thought arises do not follow it but enquire, for whom is this thought? is a thought. 'To me' is a thought'. 'Who am I? is a thought. 'Be Still' is a thought. 'Be Still' and know that 'I Am - whether thought is or is not'.

Dr. MK: The power of positive thinking is a famous concept. Norman Vincent Peale wrote a series of books on positive thinking and staunch belief. There is a story that goes like this. Once a poor factory worker was injured in his left toe. Being poor, he could not miss work to attend to his toe. So, every day before going to work, he would sit in front of God and pray like this. "Dear God, you know that I am injured. Normally, when people get some defects in our products, they bring them to our factory and we repair and give them back as we are the manufacturers. Now, you are the manufacturer of my body. I cannot bring it to you for repair. I don't know how you will do it but you have to cure me." Like this, he used to pray and within a week he was cured. It was his positive thoughts and the firm belief in God that cured him.

There is another story. One small girl of 5, 6 years old used to come to the temple every morning and pray in front of God and go back smiling. The pujari observed this and wondered what this girl was murmuring every day. One day, he couldn't control himself. When the girl came and did her prayers, he called her and asked what did she pray and did she know any hymns, etc. The girl replied, "No, I don't know any prayers. But I know the alphabet from a to z. I repeat them a few times. God knows everything and He will convert these into prayers and bless me". So saying she ran away smiling. The priest was astounded at the girl's simple logic and pure untainted belief.

2. ***"We don't see things as they are, we see them as we are."***
NNK: This statement on the importance of a conscious observer is from Anais Nin, a writer and diarist whose life has led to many books and films trying to capture her philosophy in life.

It is now established by science that the senses are only a range of perceptions which allow us to see Reality only in that range. It is now known that Bats and Snakes live in a different world from each other and humans as our range of senses varies. When I identify with knowledge gathered in my mind, I also see the world differently from the senses, but as constructed by that knowledge. Thought could think of Hitler as a bad person or, if I am a Neo-Nazi, as a good person. When I use my intellect, I see the world alongside Immanuel Kant, as made up of humans, each worthy of reverence as they have Pure Reason in them, the One Source of all morality, justice, and aesthetics. When I identify with the supreme unconditional love, I see everything consumed in that Grace which is Bliss. When I enquire, 'For whom is this thought?', the 'I' is stilled. One merges all instruments of perception - senses, mind, and intellect - in that still consciousness - I Am. It is clear that I perceive the other only to the extent to which the instrument of perception allows or is allowed to. For whom is this instrument of perception? Who am I?

Dr. MK: This quote is often attributed to the Talmud, an ancient Jewish text, but its exact origin is uncertain. The meaning of this quote is that our perceptions and interpretations of the world are influenced by our own experiences, beliefs, and biases. In other words, our understanding of reality is shaped by our individual perspectives and the way we see ourselves and the world around us. This concept is often used to emphasize the subjective nature of perception and the importance of considering different viewpoints.

From my perspective, it means that many people keep seeing and saying and doing the same things again and again, and wondering why they get the same bad outcomes as they usually do. Plainly it is because they do not see things properly, meaning not entirely accurately, and in a way that should (and probably does) cause them concern. Why? Because if they are not happy with the outcomes they have experienced they are wasting their lives just repeating various errors, and most likely the same errors.

Is it possible to get past this, to avoid it entirely? Maybe, meaning yes, to some extent, and not entirely, and certainly not even that much in one bold move. Because no matter what happens, no matter how we try to avoid it, each of us will remain both filter and recipient. That much we cannot change. But there is the idea, or hope, that seeing this reality, our own participation in creating this reality, and having some awareness of it, will change how we see things and what we then do.

Second, there is a version of this idea which is that we each live in a bubble, a bubble that we create, and in which we are comfortable. We remain comfortable at some unpleasant expense, however, in terms of dealing with reality.

And this relates to the comical, ludicrous in my opinion, idea that we live in some "other" reality, a "simulation" made by some other entity, and not in the real world we see. As far as I am concerned, Plato was one of the first to consider such a situation, or at least propose to document or describe it. This so-called solution leaves us with two "realities" to explain, not just one. I do not know how anyone could consider that an improvement in terms of understanding "reality." It does change the nature of the discussion. But in the end it just adds another layer of difficulty. Is that an improvement?

The escape or justification of this idea of a filter and reality sometimes leads people to question "free will" and their own ability to change their reality. They feel they have no chance, that there is no escape, and that all is pre-ordained. And yes, that would be the case if we operate only by rules we did not make and do not understand. The outcomes will not be as we might wish, or hope, but according to the rules we have done the right thing.

Our thoughts drive our actions and behaviour. The world is as we see it and it exists like that, till we believe otherwise. The famous story of six blind men touching the elephant and each saying it is a different item comes to mind. WYSIWYG is a popular phrase that Americans use. It means – What You See Is What You Get. The perception that we have of things around us, people around us, and the world at large is tempered by our knowledge level. While we were young, we would believe it if somebody told us that that house was a haunted one and ghosts lived there. But, as we grow up and our knowledge expands, we will start laughing at the beliefs that we had when we were young.

3. ***"Personal transformation can and does have global effects. As we go, so goes the world, for the world is us. The revolution that will save the world is ultimately a personal one."***

NNK: This quote on the primary nature of personal transformation and how it is related to world transformation is from Marianne Williamson an author, speaker, and former candidate for President of the United States.

Nearly two billion years ago, there was not enough oxygen in the atmosphere to support life on Earth. There lived a bacterium called Cyano Bacteria. For its existence and survival for the 15 days that each bacteria lived, it breathed in carbon dioxide and exhaled oxygen. More than a billion years of this personal transformation transformed water, soil, and atmosphere. The oxygen level in the atmosphere increased. The ozone layer was formed 750 million years ago. Higher forms of living beings not only came into existence but also each lived for personal transformation by which each transformed the world just as each cyanobacterium did.

In the mind, however, the arrow of time and transformation can also go backward. I fall from grace when I pursue negative thoughts. I pull down my team too. So, in the sensory world there was evolution.

Now, mentally advanced beings have come and the ozone layer is under severe threat.

For whom is this individual transformation that creates team transformation for better or worse in the world as a whole? Who am I? When the 'I' is stilled is there this process of becoming? When the 'I' is stilled, is there a time or space or objective world in that still awareness-existence? When the 'I' is still, is there individuality or a sum of individualities? For whom is this thought of progress or regress? Who am I?

Dr. MK: I recollect Gandhiji's quote when I read this. He said, 'Be the change you want to see'. To me, it means that the work I do for myself, the change I hope to see and be in the world, and how I interact with the world around me...to strive to make progress, not only in who I am and how I am being...but, in asking myself, "Could I be better, clearer, more informed... about making my decisions?" and "Am I doing what is right for the greater good, or am I choosing only what my ego and convenience or comfort have dictated?"

Our scriptures do not at all advocate a fatalistic view of life, as it is often alleged. The purpose of the scriptures is to guide us to elevate, integrate, and fulfill our personality by scientifically and assiduously employing our will and effort. Bhagavad Gita highlights the role of self-effort in verse 6.5: "***Uddharet ātmanātmānam*** – Elevate yourself by your own effort".

Right from birth, we are slaves to our attraction and repulsion towards worldly objects and situations. Our mind constantly undergoes elation, depression, and agitation, depending on whether the objective situation we face is to our liking or disliking. We are fearful of losing what we like and facing what we dislike.

Bhagavad Gita wants us to transform this slavery into mastery by cultivating the "Yoga" attitude. It defines "Yoga" as evenness (**samatva**) of the mind towards success and failure, desired and undesired outcomes:

"siddhy-asiddhyoḥ samo bhūtvā samatvaṁ yoga ucyate"

(Bhagavad Gita 2.48).

And it says that remaining well seated in this yoga-attitude or *samatva*-attitude is the key to excellence in all our performances: *"yogaḥ karmasu kauśalam"* (Bhagavad Gita 2.50).

Cultivation of *samatva* means freeing the mind from the clutch of *"rāga-dvesha"* – affinity and hatred. Rāga means colour. Our vision is coloured by our constricted notion of 'me' and 'mine', and the resulting likes and dislikes, preferences, and prejudice. Removal of this colour allows us to see the world as it is, and also to see ourselves as we are. The true vision enables us to perform our best in any situation.

Each of us has within us all that we will ever need. Looking outside ourselves for answers and validation will only bring more doubt...and the true question will remain unanswered..."What do I really want?" ...it is, quite honestly, not always the easiest answer to find...but it offers the most promising threshold. ...what may be the most compelling path...

4. ***"Quantum physics tells us that nothing that is observed is unaffected by the observer. It means that everyone sees a different truth because everyone is creating what they see."***

NNK: This quote attempting to connect modern science and spirituality, is from Neale Donald Walsch, an American author who has written the series 'Conversations with God'.

We were a team of eight trying to support one of the eight in her journey to happiness. When I discussed various points of view and faced steady disagreement, I would sometimes slip into saying that the rest of the members, all the seven of us who had taken up this service of giving support to her, agreed on the issue and she alone was not seeing the point. Here, it may be pertinent to see that the seven, including me, were supposed to be placed by her to be in a better state of happiness if not sharpness of intellect. She would counter by saying that the entire humanity was wrong on many issues for centuries before correcting itself. So, why couldn't the seven of them be wrong?

I realised that the receiving intellect had veto power against any suggestion. In quantum physics, the observer, as observation itself in any form is a form of measurement, seems to affect the observed. He is really creating his own reality or seeing what he wants to see. In revealing the Viswa Roopa Darshana or Cosmic vision, Sri Krishna says to Arjuna, 'See what you want to see'. This brings power and responsibility to the observer.

What is it in the observer that allows him to see the same circumstances as an impossible hurdle or an incredible opportunity? What is it that allows Kant to suggest that let each man frame his own moral rules and live by them, he is bound to find the source of morality? For whom is this thought? Who am I who has this ability to see whatever I want to see? When the ego is still, all measurements are in abeyance. Is the source, not one, undivided being consciousness? Is there a division between an observer and observed in that being-consciousness?

DR. MK: This is a very deep statement. The observed, the observer, and the perception are all distinct. But quantum physics states that anything that has not been observed has yet to come into existence. This is called the "Observer Effect". But the Universe does not need any observer to exist. So is the case with truth. It is. That's all. But does our behaviour change because we are being 'observed'? Absolutely. Right from the student's behaviour in the examination hall when the invigilator is there, to a prisoner behaving subdued when watched by security, we do change our behaviour when we are observed. It again gets deeper. The observed does not have to change. From this new situation, a question of purely metaphysical nature emerged, about the nature of the reality in which we live, and more specifically about the validity of the hypothesis of *realism*, which until then had been widely shared by most physicists and philosophers of science.

Roughly speaking, we can define the idea of realism as the hypothesis that **"there is a reality out there,"** whose existence is entirely *independent* of the observing subjects, and that this reality, precisely because it exists autonomously, would be knowable and describable in an *objective* way, for example through the construction of appropriate scientific theories. To put it in more suggestive terms, according to the view of realism, it would always be possible, at least in principle, to speak about reality regardless of the mind of the observing subject who studies and contemplates it.

5. ***"The quieter you become, the more you will be able to listen and learn."***

NNK: These are the words of Rumi. To listen and learn is at the heart of life. Unless the consciousness within listens and learns, it stagnates or even slips down.

If one is impulsive in speech, listening and learning are out of the question. Tiruvalluvar, the great poet-saint comes in with the need to hold the tongue. When one is observant of one's impulse to speak, one can listen. Listen to others. Listen to the world. Listen to the wind. Listen to one's own breath. Listen to one's own thoughts.

One learns how one is impulsive in thought and enslaved to thought. For whom is this thought? Who am I? The root impulse to rise as a separate ego is addressed and eliminated. One understands that the root of misery is to feel separated from the rest. One learns that it is all one family - ***Vasudaiva Kutumbakam***. It is one Self. Quieten the tongue, breath, mind, intellect, and ego. Directly quieten or still the ego. To such a one, life teaches everything. Nay! One learns from life which is always teaching everyone.

Dr. MK: The phrase "the quieter you become, the more you can hear" is often attributed to the spiritual leader Ram Dass, and it is often used to suggest that when one is quiet and still, both physically and mentally, they will be able to hear things that they may have missed when they were busy and distracted. This can refer to both external sounds and internal thoughts, and it is often used as a reminder to take a moment to be quiet and reflective, to gain deeper understanding and insight.

There are points in our lives when we are in the midst of change, stuck in turmoil, perhaps finding ourselves at a crossroads. The moment, when we feel overwhelmed, numb, lost. The moment when we find ourselves, asking "Who am I?". The days when we feel unrest and a tug at our heart. For some it's far too easy to ignore this tug, to go through the motions, to "just make it by". For others, the tug, the yearning is a sign, a sign that there is a bigger message and meaning out there ready to be heard, if we choose to make time to listen.

Making it a daily priority to be still, be quiet, to listen enables us to hear the voice. The voice of the universe, the voice of God - guiding us through this turmoil. The turmoil that one day will blossom into an amazing transformation - the transformation leading us to our true selves, who we were meant to be.

6. ***"When you see yourself in others, and all others in you, it is impossible to hurt anyone else or be hurt by the world ".***

NNK: This idea emanates from the Bhagavad Gita.

When we see ourselves in others, we do not hurt them. When we see ourselves in the irritated elder troubled by old age, one responds with compassion. When one sees oneself in the hungry street dog, one brings out the biscuits in the bag. When one sees oneself in the drooping plant facing the mid-day Sun without water for many days like the sage Vallalar, one not only does not hurt but heals.

However, modern psychology reveals that one could cause oneself serious self-injury if one merely is subservient to the troubles of others. Eventually, such menial behaviour leads to an injured and injurious personality. That is why one has to see all others in oneself. Not only am I in the elderly but the elderly person who was comforted is in me. The dog who received food is in me. The plant when watered and swaying happily is in me. Then one serves others and receives the service oneself. There is no self-injury. There is no helping or injuring another self.

Are there two selves? For whom is this thought of seven billion others? For whom is this thought of the other? Who am I? One finds oneself in others and all others in oneself.

Dr. MK: In verse 6.32 of the Bhagavad Gita, Lord Krishna is describing who is a superior yogi. He has stated, *"One who sees a similarity between self and all living entities, that a yogi is considered superior."* What is empathy? It is the ability to understand another person's feelings and experiences, especially because you have been in a similar situation.

It is somewhat different from the more common emotion — sympathy, which is defined as the feeling of being sorry for somebody; showing that you understand and care about somebody's problems. While sympathy is the feeling of pity or sorrow for someone else, empathy is the ability to emotionally understand what other people feel, see things from their point of view, and imagine yourself in their place. That is the reason empathy is a divine quality worthy of mention by the Lord. In the same verse, Lord Krishna goes further and says that yogi should be able to do so whether in pleasure or pain. Most people, who do possess the quality of empathy do so in good time.

But if one can show empathy towards others, God is pleased, because it shows that one is treating others as equal souls, who are prone to err as all of us are. You show empathy to a fellow being and see how quickly you begin to see the good side of his personality. Don't we all possess both good and bad emotions? Yes, the classification of a good person and a bad one is based on the preponderance of them, not the absence of them. So as long as you empathize with others, you can knowingly not hurt them.

7. ***"You have to grow from the inside out. None can teach you, none can make you spiritual. There is no other teacher but your own soul."***

NNK: These awakening words are from Swamy Vivekananda.

The source of learning and growth keeps getting tossed about between the outside and the inside. Are parents the cause for my downfall? We were four children and the other three are good, if not great, in their conduct. So, the cause for learning and growth is within.

Psychologists in the U.S.A. took statistics as their grounding knowledge and concluded that delinquency happened with divorced parents and a hurtful upbringing. They could no longer be uplifted but only medicated into not creating trouble. Two mindfulness meditators adopted some of these children and gave them non-intrusive love. The new neurons generated every day changed by epigenetic response to that love and the children uplifted themselves. Was the love from outside the key?

In the meditation hall in Ramana Ashram, one can feel the overwhelming peace quieten the soul. But why does it quieten me better now than before? I can feel that peace. So, sensitivity to that influence, even though it is of the highest order, is within me. For whom is this thought that I am quiet? Who am I? The spark is inside the child. As a teacher, be a mere enabler for the child to bring that light from the inside out and be a light to oneself and the world.

Dr. MK: When you adopt the habit of introspection, your soul becomes your true teacher. There is no better teacher than your own soul. It guides you through ups and downs, making you a better person along the way. This teaching also implies the importance of self-belief. The ones who believe in themselves are the ones who are successfully able to grow from the inside out, and not vice versa. The ones who listen to their soul are the ones who have unwavering belief in their capabilities. They do not seek external affirmation as their soul guides them through everything.

There is a beautiful story from Mahabharata. It was the time when Pandavas & and Kauravas were living in *Gurukula*, serving *Dronacharya*. They'd do menial jobs like sweeping the floor, bringing sticks from the forest for cooking, or begging for alms. Drona was also happy as he was able to inculcate some good habits among the future kings.

Once Drona wanted to take the test of ethics. He thought that he would ask different questions and based upon the answers of his disciples he would give them some lessons to memorize. This way, as per the individual pace of the student, Drona will teach them the laws of ethics. So, in the beginning, he gave them certain lessons to memorize. On the day of examination, Drona quizzed all the 105 brothers. Everyone was ready as they wanted to impress their teacher. Drona asked very simple questions like whether one should speak a lie. Everyone gave wonderful answers but alas! Yudhishthira was unable to respond. Drona thought that maybe he didn't get time to memorize the lesson. He gave Yudhishthira another week to memorize.

Next week, when Drona met Yudhishthira, he asked him the same question.

"So tell me Yudhishthira, should we tell a lie or not?" Drona asked.

"Gurudeva I am afraid but I don't know the answer to this question." Yudhishthira's head bowed in shame.

"How is this possible my dear Son? This is a simple yes or no answer. Still, if you are unable to memorize it, then I will give you three more days." Drona said worriedly.

The next three days were visibly painful for Yudhishthira. He was worried about how to answer Gurudev's question. Drona was also observing his disciple and was worried about him. How can Yudhishthira, who is the noblest of all the brothers, not answer this simple question? At the end of 3 days, Drona again asked the question, "Should we lie or not?"

"No Gurudeva, we should not lie," said Yudhishthira confidently.

Drona was happy but also curious. What took the prince so long to memorize this simple lesson? He asked Yudhishthira about the same. Yudhishthira replied:

"Gurudeva, when you earlier asked me to memorize this fact, I was not sure about its authenticity. On the one hand, I would have told that one should never lie but on the other hand, I myself was lying in day-to-day life. Hence, I doubted that is it even possible to follow this injunction."

"However, in the past 10 days, I tried to become more honest. I tried not to speak lies & present myself as I am. In this way, I found peace and contentment. I found that I am not a fake person anymore. Hence, I was finally able to answer your question in the positive."

Hearing this, Drona praised Yudhishthira, saying that you are the personification of Dharma. One of the aspects of Dharma is Satyam & only an honest person can actually follow Dharma.

This shows how important it is for spiritual practitioners to internalize the scriptures. Great souls like Yudhishthira take days to finally accept a simple code of morality. Can't we at least take a few readings of the scriptures to assimilate this greatest knowledge?

8. ***"Your value does not decrease based on someone else's inability to see your worth."***

NNK: This liberating idea is from Richard Feynman a theoretical physicist who received the Nobel Prize in 1965.

Just taken literally, the quote appears to brush aside criticism. By showing that you need not be affected by another's opinion of you, he tries to liberate one from putting oneself down unnecessarily. However, we can see ourselves in others and others within ourselves. When we see ourselves in others, we do not hurt or criticise others. When we see the criticism and the critic as thoughts within ourselves, we can see what Rudyard Kipling means in saying,

"If you can trust yourself when all men doubt you, but make allowance for their doubting too;"

When we see the others and the criticism of us as within us, we can examine and provide for that doubt and really trust ourselves.

Moreover, for whom is this thought of the criticism and the critic? Who am I? The ego and all others are unified in the One Self of all. Such a one who has unified all life in the one Self within comes out to work not for getting happiness or contentment or trust from others. Such a one comes out to work happily without expecting anything. In fact, one does not go outside oneself.

Dr. MK: In our daily monotonous lives, we keep hearing the word 'value' many times in different contexts. Value for money, persons' value, etc., etc… But when it comes to oneself, we sometimes look out for someone else to endorse, appreciate, and respect us for our value – or what we think is our value.

But, let us for a minute pause and think what do we really have? Sometimes, I have doubted my value – to the organisations where I had worked, to my family, my social circle, etc. I keep wondering, 'Am I really valuable to these?'.

Now think about that. Just because someone sees something differently does not mean you need to adjust the way you perceive yourself. Who knows why that judgment might be different? It could be because you have different points of reference, varying experiences, or incongruent expectations. In fact, no two people see things the same, so there's always going to be a conflict. But speaking of the problem at hand here, this newfound information should not make you less confident in the value you offer.

Do you know why? Because we approach life from our own lens, with our own points of reference, our own experiences, built out of our own expectations. It's not practical to think that someone else knows how much value you add through your life because they didn't live it! But you did, and that's worth everything.

Besides, what if the opposite was true? What if someone said that you were worth more than you believed to be true? You'd probably resort to your own interpretation because they don't see the full picture. Well, when that's true on the negative feedback side, it shouldn't be any different on the other.

9. *"Every act of conscious learning requires the willingness to suffer an injury to one's self-esteem. That is why young children, before they are aware of their own self-importance, learn so easily; and why older persons, especially if vain or important, cannot learn at all."*

NNK: These wise words are from Thomas Szasz a psychiatrist and social thinker.

When I learn something, I must first accept that I did not know something or that I was wrong about something. Accepting, even within oneself, one's ignorance or one being in the wrong is an injury to one's self-esteem. This injury arises from self-importance. Instead of realising how oneself is a part, an intricately woven but infinitely small part, of an incredibly huge mechanism, one feels one is so important. Children do not have this self-importance and are natural learners. With the evolution of humans into intellectual beings, this too is under test as children develop self-importance very early.

The fact is that we are all connected to and dependent on, the rest. Our body is made of stardust that formed in the birth and death and reassembling of stars. Our breath owes its existence to a small bacterium that lived merely for 15 days but in over a billion years of striving, created the ozone layer. Our mind is connected with the rest of humanity through the collective subconscious. Whatever we know, we owe it to that collective library of knowledge within. When one has effaced self-importance, the learning that we are all one comes through. For whom is this thought? Who am I? When the separative self is erased at its source, the Self of all, the one undivided consciousness reveals itself. Such a one takes life wondrously and happily as the world is approached with a sense of ever-newness. The self-realised one is said to be like a child in his innocence, but consciously innocent as he is abiding in the unborn, undivided, unknowable oneness of all.

Dr. MK: Consciousness is when our minds are in a state of complete awareness. This contrasts with unconsciousness, which occurs when we do not realize that we are having certain thoughts or feelings. A large majority of human brain functions are unconscious, meaning that we are not aware of it.

Conscious learning takes place when we are engaged in the learning process. When a child is learning long division, they are, typically, learning consciously. They are watching their teacher, listening, writing down numbers, and completing math calculations in their mind. All of these skills require complete awareness or consciousness of what is happening. Unconscious learning, on the other hand, happens without our realization of it. Typically, a developing baby unconsciously learns how to roll over, for example. Unconscious learning often occurs as the result of mimicry. But to learn and make use of that knowledge is where humans make mistakes.

10. ***"Your only obligation in any lifetime is to be true to yourself. Being true to anyone else or anything else is not only impossible but the mark of a fake messiah."***

NNK: Being true to oneself is acting in a way that agrees with one's beliefs and values. These words of awakening are from Richard Bach the aviator, writer, and philosopher who wrote Jonathan Livingston Seagull and Illusions: The Adventures of a Reluctant Messiah. His philosophy is that our apparent physical limits and mortality are merely appearance. Here, he is saying that one can only be true to oneself.

This is in accord with Kantian philosophy that each one of us is worthy of respect as we have pure reason within us which allows us to frame our own beliefs and values. By being true to our own beliefs and values and acting in accord with them, we come to the truth that everyone is worthy of dignity as this pure reason is present within each. This also means that it is impossible to be true to another unless each one moves in accord with oneself. When one is true to oneself, one can and will respect the ability of each to find that pure reason within, in their own unique way. So, it is enough if one is true to oneself. One recognises this truth available to everyone and does not try to force others into their own path but only point to this freedom to follow their own beliefs and values.

In self-enquiry, one understands how being true to oneself prepares one to come to the pure, undivided reason present within each being. One finds the truth of the undivided pure reason within, beyond the apparent physical limits and mortality, which are mere appearances.

Dr. MK: Truth is the representation of Purity. With the task of upholding his father's word, Shri Ram leaves for the forest. When one follows truth with a pure heart, it becomes an inspiration for others to follow it too. The same happens with Bharat. Before leaving for the forest, Shri Ram wholeheartedly gives the kingdom to Bharat. But Bharat with a pure heart, refuses to become king and stands for the truth. Bharat reinstates the truth to Queen Kaikeyi that it is only Shri Ram who is the actual heir of the kingdom imposes upon himself self-exile, and leads his life just as his brothers lead in the forest.

Truth is the greatest weapon one has. When one follows truth, his virtue becomes his strength and this is proved by Lakshman. For Lakshman, Shri Ram's service is his greatest truth and belief. This trait gives him the strength to fight Indrajeet. With a simple but strong statement that if Shri Ram always speaks the truth, and he has served his brother truthfully, he aims the arrow of truth at Indrajeet which kills him. Such is the strength of truth.

Integrity shines in truth. Mata Sita shows that a truthful woman is the strongest of all. The love for Shri Ram is the ultimate truth of her life, and she believed in it at all times. When she is asked to go through the trial of fire, it is the same truth that supports her and delivers her again back safely into the hands of Shri Ram.

It was not only for the purpose of subduing Ravan that Shri Ram was born, but also for the purpose of making mankind follow truth as a trait of life. He proved the same through the situations he faced in life as the greatest examples. Ramayana is a reflection of truth and Shri Ram is an inspiration for us to walk on the path of truthfulness, and that remains the eternal truth in all time.

But how to be true to oneself? Is there a secret formula? Marissa Hankasson proposes ten ways to be your genuine self as follows:

1. Be honest with yourself about what you think, feel, want, and need.
2. Freely share your thoughts and feelings.

3.   Honour your needs and say no to requests that conflict with them.
4.   Accept that some people like you, and others do not, and you're okay with it. In other words, don't be a people pleaser.
5.   Surround yourself with people who respect and support you just as you are.
6.   Focus more on your core values than what society deems acceptable.
7.   Listen to your intuition and trust you know what's best for yourself.
8.   Do what feels right for you, even if it means risking approval from those around you.
9.   Allow yourself to change your mind if you recognize you made a choice that was not right for you.
10.   Allow yourself to evolve and let go of what you have outgrown.

11.   ***"Before you talk, listen. Before you react, think. Before you criticise, wait. Before you pray, forgive. Before you quit, try."***
NNK: These words emphasising self-attention are from William Arthur Ward, a motivational writer from the United States of America.

In a conversation, before speaking, one has to be self-attentive in listening. If listening does not precede speech, such words become unrelated to the feelings expressed by the other or others. As each thought is perceived in many ways by different people, one should listen to how the previous expression of ours has been viewed before responding. One could have explained an artistic object or a movie sequence as to its nuances, but the other person, your sister, might have started remembering from her family experiences which the same object of art and your words triggered. You may have the impulse to expound more about art and wax eloquent, but it will be better to walk with the sister's memory that went back fifty years when you were walking with her and your attentive father on an evening stroll.

Before reacting to circumstances, self-attention requires that one should think. Otherwise, one is merely a puppet triggered by circumstances. To observe that one is reacting or about to react with anger or excitement, to look at oneself and think appropriately, breaks the chain of puppetry, at least to a degree. One's possibility of relative freedom and absolute depends on this critical act of self-observation.

Criticism is an impulse that not only makes one a puppet triggered by circumstances but also a source of negative energy in the story going on out there. One hurts the presenter and possibly many readers or listeners. Before criticising, self-attention requires that one wait.

Before praying to God or life, there is something I can do myself. If my prayers are aimed at hurting people who have wronged me, I can forgive them. The moment I do this, I see life forgiving me of many memories of times when I have hurt others knowingly and unknowingly.

Before quitting on impulse, self-attention asks one to stop and try again. For whom is this habit of speaking without listening? Who am I? Direct self-attention takes one to the source of life where one clearly understands the significance of this message from William Arthur Ward.

Dr. MK: At one point or other you've probably heard the following "You are given two ears and one mouth for a reason; to listen twice as much as you speak." It's correct, Nature has given us two ears but only one tongue, which is a tender hint that we should listen more than what we speak. But how many of us actually listen twice as much as we speak? "I never learned anything while I was talking." This is a quote that talk show host Larry King says he thinks of regularly while interviewing people. Usually, a person who won't listen properly is unable to react appropriately to a particular situation or towards a particular person, which they have to regret later.

Every one of us has felt, 'If only I had done it like this before' or 'If only I had not spoken like that to my friend', things would have been better. In hindsight, everyone is a wise person. But do we really think? Do we really listen with full attention? NO. Many of us are NOT listeners at all. In fact, most of us just 'hear' and don't 'listen'. If we do listen, then the other parts of the quote will be easier to implement. Incidentally, this quote was attributed to Ernest Hemingway by some people but it was refuted by historians. But whoever it may have been, the value of a 'pause' before action is invaluable indeed.

12. ***"Until you make peace with who you are, you will never be content with what you have."***

NNK: These words about knowing oneself are by Doris Mortman, author and activist.

I started my journey in life in earnest when I learned that life and happiness are about who I am and what I have. For years, I journeyed under the assumption that what I have is what life is all about and that it is what I have that makes me happy. Then I see people with lots of possessions, instead of being knowledgeable about life and happiness, being miserable. I see great ones keep minimum possessions and yet be fulfilled and happy. Moreover, in deep sleep, I seem to be without any possessions, but whoever I am in deep sleep, I am fulfilled and happy indeed.

I realise that who I am is far more important, in being fulfilled and happy, than what I have. I realise that my boss at work almost forty years ago, N. S. Balasubramanian, had something important when he called me over to his cabin and shared his heart with that young man as to how being principled and ethical was more important than the post one held. He even shared his experience of how he would be courageous when all others cowered before an aggressive boss. But that did not sink into the conscious 'me' at that time. Unless one is at peace with who one is, there is absolutely no way to be content with what one has. The unethical one can never find fulfillment even from being the President of a country that possesses great material wealth. But who am I? Am I this assembly of body parts? Am I a banker, father, mother, good person, or some other identity of the mind? When a thought arises to make one identify with body and mind, one should not follow that thought. One should enquire, 'For whom is this thought? Who am I? The limited me may fall into discontentment, but, when I enquire 'Who am I?', I do not limit myself to knowing. The unknowable doesn't need any possessions to be content. Why limit oneself to a body or mind identity when the truth of the source is infinite, beyond the limited body or mental identity?

Dr. MK: Paulo Coelho once said, "Make peace with your past so it won't destroy your present." There are many things that most of us want to keep hidden from ourselves and the people around us, things that cause us so much pain and suffering. You need to realise that making peace with oneself is the most difficult thing to do. Everyone has gone through good times and bad. And if we want to move forward, we must learn to let go of the past and accept who we are. Rather than letting our past determine our future, we should learn from our past and use the experience to make us stronger, wiser, and more resilient in our lives.

The truth is that if we choose to do nothing, ignore our dark experiences, and if we don't heal our wounds, our past will continue to haunt us and put a limit on our future. To move forward and to live a successful life, we must learn to take control of our past rather than letting our past determine who we are.

Self-sabotage is one of the most common side effects that people will have if they do not heal their past and choose to go on. When an opportunity presents itself, people will consider it from their experience. If they do not have a good experience, they will choose to abandon the opportunity. On the other hand, if they had a great experience, they will go ahead with the opportunity that appears.

Thus, you must learn how to make peace with yourself if you want to live a successful and happy life. It is just like driving a car, if you want to go forward faster and farther, you must release the handbrakes. Most people drive with their handbrakes on, where their pasts are dragging them and limiting them. You simply have to release the handbrakes to go smoother, farther, and faster.

13. ***"If you are patient in one moment of anger, you will escape a hundred days of sorrow": Bombay High Court.***
   The demon in you may awake for a single moment or then you may have reached that penultimate stage where you can ignore and forgive, This was opined by the court, in the recent matter of Pravin Khimji Chauhan v. The State of Maharashtra (year 2022)"

NNK: This simple but profound insight into human behaviour was made by Justice Smt. Sadhana S. Jadhav & Justice Prithviraj K. Chavan. The accused had killed his wife in a moment of anger arising out of doubting her. The judges are wise in not only recognising the danger of yielding to anger but also showing clearly that the moment of anger is also the possibility of being the penultimate moment before, out of self-observation, one lets go of anger and decides to ignore the matter and forgive.

One moment of anger had resulted in the loss of the life of a loved companion of so many years. As the accused had surrendered and showed immense remorse, the case was reduced to culpable homicide. But, still, that moment of anger resulted in ten years imprisonment. How important it is to free oneself of one moment of anger, hatred, jealousy, shame, and other negative emotions. Each of these moments causes years to be lost. Even when one is under the sway of positive emotions like excitement, elation, intense pleasure, and group revelry, one's judgement is severely impaired. One makes commitments, decisions, and actions leading to injury and loss of years.

For whom is this positive or negative emotion? Self-attention frees one from being enslaved by emotions and the positive and negative thoughts that are at the root of emotions. Unless one is aware of oneself clearly, one is acting compelled by impulses created by thoughts and emotions.

Dr. MK: We have always been taught that anger leads to chaos and problems. In the Bhagavad Gita, in Chapter 2 verse 63, Sri Krishna says

> **krodhad bhavati sammohah sammohat smriti-vibhramah**
> **smriti-bhranshad buddhi-nasho buddhi-nashat**
> **pranashyati**

Anger leads to clouding of judgment, which results in bewilderment of memory. When memory is bewildered, the intellect gets destroyed; and when the intellect is destroyed, one is ruined.

When the intellect is clouded, it leads to bewilderment of memory. The person then forgets what is right and what is wrong, and flows along with the surge of emotions. The downward descent continues from there, and bewilderment of memory results in the destruction of the intellect. And since the intellect is the internal guide, when it gets destroyed, one is ruined. In this manner, the path of descent from divinity to impiety has been described as beginning with contemplation of the sense objects to the destruction of the intellect.

According to The Gita, Object leads to attachment, attachment leads to craving, craving leads to anger, anger leads to lack of judgement, and lack of judgement leads to the bewilderment of memory, and that leads to loss of intelligence. How beautifully the result of anger is explained. In chapter 16 verse 21, Gita says anger is considered a gateway to hell.

14. ***"Within you, there is a stillness and sanctuary to which you can retreat at any time and be yourself.."***

NNK: This guidance of deeply spiritual significance is from Hermann Hesse who was a German-Swiss poet, novelist, and painter. His best-known works include Demian, Steppenwolf, Siddhartha, and The Glass Bead Game, each of which explores an individual's search for authenticity, self-knowledge, and spirituality.

In this quote, he is addressing the inner stillness within each one of us which is available as a sanctuary. It is revealed by Carl Sagan that when a three-dimensional being wants to speak to a two-dimensional being living in a two-dimensional world having only length and breadth but no height, to the two-dimensional being, the words will appear to come from within itself. So, all higher dimensions are to be accessed within ourselves as outside of us is the sensory world limited to three dimensions.

Within us, in the inner dimensions, the sanctuary he refers to cannot be the changing emotions or the fast-moving thoughts. When the individual, understanding the constant changes of the outer world, and the inner worlds of emotions and thoughts, stills the ego by understanding that everything is changing and one cannot do anything about this, the 'I' is still. That stillness is the divine sanctuary that Hesse is referring. This 'still I' is what Hermann Hesse refers to as 'you can be yourself'.

Whenever a thought arises, inviting attention to go to the outside world or emotions or abstract thought, one should not follow them, but enquire, 'For whom is the thought? Who am I?'. This stills the 'I' and erases the impulse to leave the stillness present inside. When all impulses are erased, this stillness is realised as the eternal rest or **Parandhama** referred to in spiritual paths. Whenever serving the world empties one's reservoir of peace, one can return to this eternal source. Ramana Maharshi, of course, says that this stillness is the only reality to be abided in.

DR. MK: Here, Stillness; means calm, quiet, and being in one's position.

Sanctuary means staying in one place and knowing, just like one visiting any holy place, but staying in peace, within one's own soul.

*Retreat; (*according to the following line) means return.

The quote means that when one is calm and at peace in their soul and mind, they can return to the place where they belong, whenever they want. All one is imagination and bring extent to own way, by this that one can bring up their morale and spirit. This quote is said for people when they are hasty and cannot do things right as planned, for them to calm down and resolve what they need to do. We grow up in an environment of overstimulation, short-lived triggers, and a complete focus on externalities. Because of all of this, for many, life becomes very messy.

Maybe you have a deeper sense that Life, in its essence, could also be very simple. Maybe you have experiences of this simplicity. But how many times have you actually experienced this? Felt the joy of life run through your veins like a Kenyan Marathon runner on speed. By just sitting still and going within.

There is only one key to this, and it seems that Hermann Hesse found that key. It is finding peace deep within ourselves. It is embarking on the journey to that inner sanctuary as he magically calls the space where silence can be found.

If it was all so simple, we would be blissfully happy, dancing our way to work on Monday mornings, hugging everybody we meet, floating on our inner unstoppable volcano of joy and all would meditate during our lunch break.

In reality, one of the most difficult things to practice, for many people, if not all, is becoming silent. Can you sit still and quiet your mind even for 10 minutes? To reach that vast infinite sea of time deep within your soul. It is there for you always, like a calm lake. You are that stillness, you are the lake. Never forget this.

Meditate. Reconnect with nature. Become silent. There are a million ways. Find your own.

15. ***"The greatest good you can do for another is not just to share your riches but to reveal to him his own."***

NNK: These words on serving others are from a former Prime Minister of Great Britain, who served for two terms during the 19th Century, Benjamin Disraeli. This is, perhaps a sophisticated way of restating the saying, 'It is better to teach a man to fish rather than just give him fish'.

In the year 2000, one of my friends from the 1990s had come to Bangalore leaving a lucrative practice of document writing in a Taluk headquarters as he had lost heavily in the stock market. He had not only lost his funds but also the funds of others who had entrusted their savings to him. When I met him, I was practising meditation as learned from Shankar Mutt, Kanchipuram. I shared with him that he should steady his mind by the ***Gayatri Mantra*** that he liked, but felt he would not believe my words unless I gave him some money which he had asked me for. I was not totally dependent on the power of meditation myself hence this slip. The money I gave was lost in a week in the stock market. The next tranche too met the same fate. I asked for some money from home the next time he came as I had run out of personal funds. I saw the pain in the face of the hardworking homemaker and realised my mistake. I had not understood the power of the mind. He had not changed the nature of his mind and had lost all of Rs 13,000/- in no time. I refused his request and told him that working on his mind alone was enough. I met him five years later, happily living in a job role he could easily discharge and with finances in order.

First, one has to understand the limitless treasure within oneself. The only way to serve others, as pointed out by Benjamin Disraeli, is to point out and help bring out this inner treasure in each one. In self-enquiry, one is revealed the limitless treasure of the Self of all within.

Dr. MK: True wealth is not a function of your bank account, a fleet of cars, an array of gold and jewelry, but your ability to raise others to the full awareness of what they carry inside.

The story of Michael Faraday and how he rose from being a janitor to a giant in the field of electrochemistry, also testifies to the fact that how we help others realise their full potential is a strong determinant of our own worth.

Faraday was a janitor in the laboratory of the Royal Institution in Great Britain under Sir Humphrey Davy, who saw in Faraday, an 'image' that goes beyond an ordinary janitor. Humphrey trained the man who later taught the world how to convert chemical energy into power and light.

When Humphrey was asked what his greatest discovery was, and despite having several inventions and patents to his credit, the great mentor said confidently: "My greatest discovery is Michael Faraday." In fact, history has it, that the only school Faraday went to was a Sunday School. Imagine a man without formal education teaching professors and scholars of his time how to generate electricity.

In the current times too, we have heard of real-life stories of Zoho Corporation in Tamil Nadu, and how they transformed the lives of ordinary village children into software engineers and marketing specialists by educating them, guiding them, and mentoring them. The dedication of Sridhar Vembu, the founder of Zoho, and his team is immense.

Mentoring is definitely the highest form of education. Isaac Newton said: "If I have seen farther than others, it is because I was standing on the shoulders of giants." Behind every successful person, there is a mentor who helped him along the way. Some of the most influential people in history were encouraged to succeed by some of the most well-known people of their time.

Socrates mentored Plato, Plato mentored Aristotle and Aristotle mentored Alexander the Great. Alexander the Great actually broke the loop, because when he was supposed to be mentoring youth and building people, he was busy building empires and accumulating riches. He died without investing in others and his legacies also died with him.

Mark Twain said: "Keep away from people who try to belittle your ambitions. Small people always do that, but the really great make you feel that you, too, can become great. When you are seeking to bring big plans to fruition, it is important with whom you regularly associate."

One audacious step unleashed the giant in the young boy, who later changed the face of tech gadgets. That summer job and close mentoring from Hewlett changed Steve Jobs' life forever. Jobs was young, green, and inexperienced, living in Mountain View, California, and had found Hewlett's number in the phone book.

As Steve Jobs later recounted in an emotional interview in 1994: "He didn't know me at all, but he ended up giving me some parts and he got me a job that summer working at Hewlett-Packard, working on the assembly line, putting nuts and bolts together on frequency counters… I was putting in screws. It didn't matter; I was in heaven."

The blessing of influence is in helping others succeed. Until you become an integral part of other people's success stories, you are just merely existing. Use the platform, experience, exposure, and riches you have to build others up. Always look for a way to lift someone up and if that is all you do, it is enough. The truth is that the more you lift others up, the more the Almighty raises you.

16. ***Detachment is not that you should own nothing, but that nothing should own you.***"

NNK: This foundational statement of spiritual practice which supports all spiritual practices is from Alī ibn Abī Ṭālib who was the last Caliph of the Rashidun Caliphate, the successor state to the Islamic prophet Muhammad's political dominions. He is considered by Shia Muslims to be the first Imam, the rightful religious and political successor to Muhammad.

Detachment is the basis of liberty. Detachment from the limited is the way to free consciousness to find its inherent freedom and bliss in eternity. All the mystical teachings too have detachment as the core of mystical experience. There is a German mystic who exclaimed that out of all the spiritual practices he has studied in a thousand years of religious and philosophical thought till then, detachment was the closest to God. Detachment creates a space in the individual where God or the supreme spirit alone can enter.

In Indian spiritual teachings, there is a mantra on victory over death of all limited existence through detachment of all limited relationships, with great gentleness, just as a ripe cucumber fruit lying on Mother Earth will gently separate itself from the mother vine so gently so as to not hurt the vine or itself. Here, the suggestion is that detachment is not that you should not own anything but that those objects and relationships should not own you. Coming from a caliph, it is like king Janaka of yore who was said to be a Jnani, who is one in the supreme spirit, though he was the great king of much of India of his times.

There is a story that when an invitee saint and King Janaka were discussing in his palace, the building catches fire and both the saint and King run out of the palace. The king ran out nonchalantly leaving all his wealth as though nothing was lost while the saint rushed back to his room to pick up his books and clothing which were precious to him.

In self-enquiry, as each thought arises, one should look at it with detachment and let it go. One should hold the 'I' with the quest 'Who am I?', till all impulses creating attachment to the limited objects and relationships are completely erased and complete detachment shines as unconditional love towards all. Complete detachment from limitations and complete freedom of consciousness are the same, says Ramana Maharshi.

Dr. MK: In fact, as is so often the case with the big issues of spiritual life, detachment involves a deep paradox. It's true that those without a lot of clutter in their lives have more time for inner practice. But in the long run, disengaging ourselves from family, possessions, political activism, friendships, and career pursuits can actually *impoverish* our inner lives. Engagement with people and places, skills and ideas, money and possessions is what grounds inner practice in reality.

The Bhagavad Gita, which is surely the basic text on the practice of detachment, is wonderfully explicit on this point. Krishna tells Arjuna that acting with detachment means doing the right thing for its own sake because it needs to be done, without worrying about success or failure. T.S. Eliot paraphrased Krishna's advice when he wrote, "For us, there is only the trying. The rest is not our business."

At the same time, Krishna repeatedly reminds Arjuna not to cop out of doing his best in the role his destiny demands of him. In a sense, the Bhagavad Gita is one long teaching on how to act with maximum grace while under maximum pressure. The Gita actually addresses many of the questions that we have about detachment—pointing out, for instance, that we are really supposed to give up not our families or our capacity for enjoyment but our tendency to identify with our bodies and personalities instead of with pure, deathless Awareness.

Whether we're doing it daily or as a way of dealing with a big bump in our road, practicing detachment is easier if we do it with a soft attitude. I have a huge amount of respect for the Zen warrior approach to the inner life, the one in which you heroically renounce your weaknesses and tough out the hard stuff, perhaps using your sense of humor to give you the power to move forward. But when I try to detach in that way, it seems to lead to a kind of emotional deep freeze.

17. ***"To be aware of a single shortcoming within oneself is more useful than to be aware of a thousand in somebody else."***

NNK: These words of wisdom and self-awareness are from the Dalai Lama XIV who is the present Dalai Lama in 2023. The slightly expanded version in his words can be found on the internet.

"To be aware of a single shortcoming within oneself is more useful than to be aware of a thousand in somebody else. Rather than speaking badly about people in ways that will produce friction and unrest in their lives, we should practice a purer perception of them, and when we speak of others, speak of their good qualities. If you find yourself slandering anybody, first imagine that your mouth is filled with excrement. It will break you of the habit quickly enough."

The emphasis of His Holiness is not to have negative thoughts or slander others. He turns around to self-awareness by saying that one is corrupting one's own mind and speech by those faults seen in others. How will we then judge a person as it is necessary to do in worldly activities? The intelligence that can see its defect of finding fault with others is purer than the one that carries loads of negative thoughts. Such intelligence can act appropriately and let go of actions in the moment of their ending. All actions of others are taken at that moment and no one's character is permanently judged from their temporary actions. Such a one does not need to hold positive thoughts about others and oneself too. When the individual learns to let go of all thoughts, both positive and negative, he is said to live from moment to moment with the intelligence of the flow of life as a whole. In self-enquiry, one goes to the source of self-knowledge which is at the same time knowledge of the reality of others, which does not judge oneself or others.

Dr. MK: One of my ex-colleagues has *always* had issues with his coworkers and managers, no matter what company or job. But this person is also combative and disagreeable—so while, to him, it's always *other* people who are the problem, in reality, it's probably him.

These situations happen a lot. The unfortunate thing is that those people don't even realize they're doing it to themselves. But the more unfortunate thing is that we're doing the same things in *our* lives but we don't realise it either. You can't fix what you don't know is broken. That is why self-awareness is the most important life skill you can build.

If you want to achieve incredible heights in your life, self-awareness helps you find your weaknesses, so you can improve on them. I'm not even talking about superficial things like productivity, job skills, or fitness; I'm talking about deeper personality traits, temperament, and behaviour.

For example, someone might give off a condescending, combative vibe without knowing—over their life, it might hold them back from job promotions, life partners, happier friendships, and more. They'll always wonder why they struggle in life, but they'll never know how their behaviours or beliefs hold them back. And if you tell them about their issue, they'll deny it (or even attack you) and say that they're perfectly fine (and it's everyone *else* who's wrong).

Self-awareness can also improve the quality of your life. Because even if you have millions of dollars and travel the world in luxury, if you *still* have serious problems that are sabotaging you, you will never be free. You will always be blocked by something you aren't consciously aware of.

While some might take a few breaths or listen to soothing music to become more mindful, there's no substitute for being alone with your thoughts. It can be a surprisingly uncomfortable experience that brings up many difficult emotions. By meditating regularly, you strengthen your ability to become aware of all of your thoughts, patterns, and behaviours. When you get upset, you can actually feel it happening within you. That way, rather than getting carried away by the emotion, you can watch it so it doesn't control you, which helps you keep your peace of mind.

For example, some days I feel I'm more irritable than normal for no reason. I don't judge it; I just become aware of it so it doesn't control me. Yet if I was oblivious to it, I would just blame other things or people for "disturbing me mentally" when, in reality, it was just coming from within.

Self-awareness is difficult and, sometimes, painful. Admitting your shortcomings is hard, especially as you realize the problems it may have caused throughout your entire life without you knowing. But as Socrates wrote, "An unexamined life is not worth living."

18. ***"When we want to transform ourselves, we need to stop thinking of self and start thinking about others. This will lead to the way of transformation"***.

NNK: This quote is taken from the ideas of Joseph Campbell, an American author, mythologist, and philosopher who essentially asked one to 'Follow your Bliss'.

In my life, this idea to stop worrying about myself but look at the underlying problem of life started in a lecture to my students. Though I had developed a little empathy for others and would feel for them, my life still had my problem and my success as the centre. In that lecture, I had gathered my forty or so students who had joined me to learn about getting through a competitive exam for entering a career in Banking. My aim for that presentation was to promote a self-improvement or personality-improvement course. I had taken ideas from the Bhagavad Gita and Stephen Covey. The presentation was a great success. I was happy that I had an opportunity to learn and solve my problems while sharing what I had learned to improve myself.

A student, at the end of the presentation, asked me about fate and free will and their connection as I had used the Bhagavad Gita as one of my primary sources. On my expressing my ignorance, he suggested the teachings of J. Krishnamurthy and Ramana Maharshi. I stopped my personality development course admissions and started serious study of these teachers. The problem shifted from being a personal problem to be solved by me to the actual problem being the ego or separative feeling in all and the solution being erasing the ego. My difficulties would continue if I did not address this problem faced by all of us. In pursuing this line of penance, my individual problems got dismantled with great ease and my journey in the common turbulence of life, faced by all, began in earnest.

In self-enquiry, one directly pays attention to this false division from others present in each one of us. It takes one to the point of understanding Joseph Campbell's finding the common 'Hero's Journey' in the life of all. Self-enquiry takes one beyond the oneness of all humans. It takes one to that consciousness that is one beyond the division of 'living' and 'non-living' beings. Living and non-living arise from outward measurement of the level of consciousness expressed by a being. But self-enquiry takes one to the source of the being or existence within both 'living' and 'non-living' beings. Ramana is once known to have remarked 'Even the slab of stone you are sitting on is full of life (pure being; pure existence). One Self.

Dr. MK: Most days, most of us don't feel heroic. Just getting through our routines can seem like a mean feat. But what if you could become more awesome without doing anything extreme—simply transforming slowly and steadily into the kind of person you idolise? What if you could be a hero?

In his 2018 book *Gradual Awakening: The Tibetan Buddhist Path of Becoming Fully Human,* contemplative psychotherapist Miles Neale argues that you can. He believes that this effort not only makes your life more meaningful but also benefits humanity.

Neale is an instructor in psychology, psychiatry, and integrative medicine at Weil Cornell Medical College in New York and a Buddhist teacher. His book lays out a training program for personal evolution that combines ancient mysticism and modern medicine, spiritual practices, neuroscience, and the insights of the acclaimed academic, mythologist Joseph Campbell.

The result is a holistic approach to a fulfilling existence. In Neale's words, "The gradual path of awakening proposes an alternative to spontaneous, all-or-nothing enlightenment, quick fixes, and New Age self-help for seekers ready to commit to the hard work, over the long haul, that it takes to become fully human."

"A hero is someone who has given his or her life to something bigger than oneself," according to Campbell's definition. Anyone can become a hero—on purpose or even accidentally. But it involves a painful evolution that is a prerequisite to greatness.

The 12 steps, as Campbell defined them, begin with a call to adventure, a challenge or quest that presents itself to an ordinary person in the ordinary world. Initially, the person is afraid and refuses that call. But with guidance from a mentor or a text, they overcome their fears, cross the threshold, and commit to the journey.

Along the way, they are tested, meet allies and enemies, and prepare for an ordeal—some kind of showdown or difficulty that will truly test their mettle. The ordeal forces them to face their worst fears. And when they survive this, the ordinary person is a hero and is rewarded, usually with knowledge or insight.

The reward's not the end of the story, however. Next, the hero must return to the ordinary world where the journey began, transformed by their experience. Finally, the reborn hero shares what he has learned on the journey, with others.

Campbell's formula is not just a way to interpret the great tales of historical and contemporary myths. It also lends meaning to our everyday existence, putting our individual struggles in a noble context. The trials and tribulations we face and survive may not seem heroic. But knowing that we grow as a result of them and that this can make us into better people, makes it easier to be brave.

19. ***"The mark of your ignorance is the depth of your belief in injustice and tragedy. What the caterpillar calls the end of the world, the Master calls the butterfly."***

NNK: This ultimate change of perspective is from Richard Bach, the author of books like Jonathan Livingston Seagull. It may appear difficult from the perspective of one who identifies with the dying. However, it is a perspective one can get by looking at life. Unless the caterpillar dies, how is the butterfly to come into existence? Unless the seed dies, how can the plant, tree, forest, the oxygen, the ozone layer, and the higher organisms be born and survive?

There is this barber who gives free haircuts to the homeless, taking time out of his business, by having a mobile set up with which he seeks out those homeless ones. Unless the time is taken out of one's self-interest, how can one, as a barber, enter the journey of giving the first free haircut to that homeless person, and begin one's journey towards unconditional love?

Without ending the known, how can one truly explore the unknown, let alone the unknowable? Unless the separate ego is diluted, how to identify with the family, state, country, all humans, or all living beings? Without dying, how to be born into the Self of all?

Dr. MK: There may come a time when you feel the call to become something more than you've always been; a call to let go of one way of living, without being clear about exactly where you are going. All you know is that you can no longer stay where you are. This is the call of the butterfly.

Life only really begins when you answer this call. It is you saying Yes to your soul, and Yes to soul-full living. It is the courageous beginning of a journey away from what no longer feeds your soul, towards a life that allows you to express yourself more fully and authentically. Answering the call awakens your life purpose from within.

For most people, answering the call of the butterfly is a gradual process. Much like a caterpillar, in time you transform your limited identity and life, and open to new realizations of your true Self and the possibilities that come to you. Your life unfolds in new and exciting ways, and you become a conscious participant in creating it.

20. ***"Why should you try to mend The failings of the world, sirs? Correct your bodies first, each one of you! Correct your minds first, each one!"***

NNK: This focus of attention on oneself as the beginning of all correction is from Basavanna, the 12th-century statesman, religious teacher, and social reformer who rejected gender and social discrimination.

This quote is selected from one of his Vachanas (poems giving spiritual and secular teachings for day-to-day living). Here, he is pointing to the need to begin reform with oneself. Though a great social reformer, he is reflecting on the truth that unless one reforms oneself, one's service to others will be from that mind-body that is impure.

Moreover, we usually forget that we ourselves are a part of creation and reform should necessarily start with oneself. There is a tweet by a modern scientist that the Universe is without compassion. It merely is rule-based. A stand-up comedian, who is well experienced in spiritual living, responds that the scientist and comedian belong to the Universe. If they, being such tiny parts of this vast universe, can be compassionate to fellow beings, how can one say that the Universe does not have compassion? In self-enquiry one seeks to find the truth of oneself in the Truth of the world. The two cannot be two different truths. Find your truth and you shall find and be the Truth of all, points out Ramana Maharshi.

Dr. MK: It is certainly worthwhile knowing how to control the mind. Lord Krishna says in the Bhagavad Gita that the mind can be controlled by constant "practice and detachment." (the Bhagavad Gita, 6.35). He says that wherever and whenever the mind wanders, due to its flickering and unsteady nature, we must bring it back under the control of the Self (the Bhagavad Gita, 6.26).

The mind is like a child; a child is attracted to everything. It wants everything but not all things are good for it. Some things are even harmful...so the parent must discipline...Sometimes the child becomes angry and cries but the parent is determined to give the best thing even if at first it seems uncomfortable to the child.

In a similar way the intelligence and the spiritual being that we are must control the mind. The mind is attracted to so many material things and everywhere we look, someone is telling us that by having one material thing or another we will be happy...but it always proves to be false.

No matter how much we get, still, we're dissatisfied. So, the mind must be disciplined, and by practice, we must learn to pull it away from those things that are not good for it. Detachment is helpful because if we can understand that real happiness comes not from material things, but rather from a loving relationship with Krishna, then we can become detached from all the pushings of material desires and we can control the mind.

21. ***"We should not feel pride in our charity, austerity, valour, scriptural knowledge, modesty, and morality, for the world is full of the rarest gems."***

NNK: This meditation on the final hurdle to liberation is by Chanakya, who was an ancient Indian polymath, active as a teacher, author, strategist, philosopher, economist, jurist, and royal advisor. He has meditated on all the four goals of life aspired for in the Hindu way of life - *dharma, artha, kama, and moksha. Dharma* is ethical living, *artha* is gathering and maintaining wealth by ethical means, *kama* is the love of one human being for another where the two minds become one and *moksha* is liberation from the transience of dharma, *artha* and *kama*.

Here, he is pointing out that factor that corrupts even the highest morality. The highest morality like charity, austerity, and ethical living are corrupted if pride is not rooted out. If one knows that he is humble, is that humility asks J. Krishnamurthy. Chanakya makes that enquiry easier by pointing out that charity, austerity, and valour, along with other great moral qualities, belong to all and no one in particular. One finds crows sharing their food charitably, the sparrow drinks but a drop and sings all day as an epitome of austerity. The mother boar chasing lions to protect her young ones is an exemplar of valour. So, have no pride in the goodness that you should necessarily have limitlessly. In self-enquiry, this pride is rooted out along with other limitations imposed on goodness.

Dr. MK: This is a beautiful message from Chanakya Neethi, chapter 14, verse 7. It states

dānē tapasi śauryē vā vijñānē vinayē nayē |
vismayō nahi kartavyō bahuratnā vasundharā ||

In the Bhagavad Gita, Chapter 16, verse 4, Sri Krishna says,

dambho darpo 'bhimānaśh cha krodhaḥ pāruṣhyam eva cha
ajñānaṁ chābhijātasya pārtha sampadam āsurīm

"Pride, arrogance, conceit, anger, harshness, and ignorance – these qualities belong to those of demoniac nature, O son of Partha."

Pride originates in the misconception that we permanently own the things that we only temporarily possess: talents and abilities, positions and possessions. Pride infatuates us with our temporary possessions and sends us off on a dangerous ego trip, being propelled by the imagination that we are superior to others and independent of Krishna.

The ride that pride takes us on is perilous from the beginning to the end. From the moment we become proud, we sentence ourselves to loneliness and insecurity. We feel lonely because our very desire for superiority alienates us from those around us as well as from Krishna. We feel insecure because of the fear that our sources of pride can and will be taken away from us at some time or the other. Hoping to get rid of the insecurity, we bury our fears by increasing our external bluff and bravado. Tragically, this only increases our loneliness, which in turn makes us more insecure, thereby activating a vicious cycle.

The ride of pride is even more perilous in the end. Why? Because when pride unceremoniously dumps us off, that is, when we lose our sources of pride, we wake up to the horrifying reality that we have hugely alienated ourselves from all those who loved us –especially Krishna.

That's why it's best to never climb aboard the ride of pride – or to get off as soon as we realize what we have got into. Gita wisdom makes this easier by offering us a far better ride: the ride back to Krishna in the plane of devotional service. Once we experience the intimacy and the security of Krishna's presence in our hearts, pride can no longer allure us.

22. ***"Negative Capability is when a man is capable of being in uncertainties, mysteries, doubts, without any irritable reaching after fact and reason"***

NNK: These words on a life of ultimate creativity are from John Keats the great English poet. The term negative capability was coined by him in a letter to his brother in the year 1817, four years before his death at the age of 25. In the letter, he introspects as to what quality went to form a 'Man of Achievement', especially in Literature, and which Shakespeare possessed so enormously. It is 'Negative Capability'. He finds this quality of Negative Capability to be the highest spiritual need in a poet.

To him, a poet has to be an exemplar of a spiritual being. Here, he is pointing to a state of mind that is 'still' in the face of the greatest uncertainty, mystery, or doubt. The mind has to be still without irritation and without moving toward fact or reason. When the poet's ego is so 'still' in negative capability, it is living without irritation in the space of the unknown. If, in the face of great uncertainty, mystery, or doubt, one moves to hold a fact known or reason through logic, one limits the unknown to the limitations of one's own individual knowledge or the knowledge of others, or even humanity as a whole. When one is so 'still' without irritability, one is without individuality and it's troubling. When Ramana Maharshi was informed of this letter on 'negative capability' by Keats, his passing remark was, 'So, there are Upanishads in English as in Sanskrit'.

In self-enquiry, the ego is directly effaced on the face of all thoughts without irritation and without reaching for another thought, however great, as a fact or reason. As soon as a thought arises as a great doubt or mystery one lets it go by enquiring, 'For whom is this thought?' If an answer comes as a fact or reason from even the greatest scriptures or thinkers, one lets go of that too without irritation by the enquiry, 'For whom is this answer?' Who am I? Be still. Be.

Dr. MK: What a wonderful thought from Keats! He is using the word 'negative' not in a pejorative sense, but to convey the idea that a person's potential can be defined by what he or she does *not* possess – in this case a need to be clever, a determination to work everything out. Essential to literary achievement, Keats argues, is a certain passivity, a willingness to let what is mysterious or doubtful remain just that.

His fellow poet Samuel Taylor Coleridge, he suggests, would do well to break off from his relentless search for knowledge, and instead contemplate on something beautiful and true ('a fine verisimilitude') caught, as if by accident, from the most secret part ('Penetralium') of mystery. The experience and intuitive appreciation of the beautiful is, indeed, central to poetic talent, and renders irrelevant anything that is arrived at through reason. Keats ends his brief discussion of negative capability by concluding that 'with a great poet the sense of Beauty overcomes every other consideration, or rather obliterates all consideration'.

Keats recognised the chameleon aspect of his own nature. He would watch sparrows from his window and peck about with them in the gravel. He would imagine the delight a billiard ball might take in its own roundness, in its smooth, rapid motion. More dramatically, he told Woodhouse how, in a room full of people, he would quickly be 'annihilated' by the different identities pressing upon him. But that was the nature of poets, of the men of genius Keats habitually measured himself against.

23. ***"Knowing your own darkness is the best method for dealing with the darknesses of other people. The healthy man does not torture others—generally, it is the tortured who turn into torturers."***

NNK: This quote on the psyche is by Carl Jung, the Swiss psychologist and psychoanalyst who founded analytical psychology.

This pointer to a deep psychological fact requires introspection. It becomes clear when we understand that all the 'good' that we see in others is also within us. When we see the 'good' in others, we are able to bring health, at least relative health, to them. When I was in deep trouble in the year 1996, a close friend of mine could see 'good' in me that no others including me could find. He put me on the clear road to recovery.

Similarly, whatever darkness or evil we see in another is in us. To that extent, we have the element of injury in us. If I am tortured by self-doubt, I disturb the self-assurance of anyone I come across. Anyone assured in his ways is a trigger for bringing up the self-doubt in me. Given the opportunity, I will threaten his assurance by bringing up doubt subtly or with force. In the process, I reinforce the self-doubt in me when the other's assurance breaks down.

The duality of 'good' and 'evil' are within us. We cast this on others. Jung calls this our 'shadow'. The injurious thoughts lie hidden in our subconscious. Even if we are 'good', it is from this unconscious or subconscious that Jung calls the collective unconscious. In self-enquiry, the duality of 'good' and 'evil' are rooted out by holding the 'I' for whom the good or evil arises. All dualities are for the 'I'. 'For whom is this thought? Who am I?', takes one to the source of the unconscious. The self-luminous Self is beyond the relative consciousness and the collective unconscious.

Dr. MK: Our mind is always playing a lot of tricks. We want to control our mind, our thoughts but the mind controls us! If we have dark thoughts in our minds, then we need to realise the same and be ready to tackle them.

The only way we can tackle our darkness is through God. In chapter 10 verse 11 of the Bhagavad Gita, Sri Krishna says,

> *teṣhām evānukampārtham aham ajñāna-jaṁ tamaḥ*
> *nāśhayāmyātma-bhāva-stho jñāna-dīpena bhāsvatā*

Out of compassion for them, I, who dwell within their hearts, destroy the darkness born of ignorance, with the luminous lamp of knowledge.

In this verse, Shree Krishna further elaborates on the concept of grace. Previously, he had explained that he bestows it upon those who lovingly absorb their minds in him and make him the paramount object of their plans, thoughts, and activities. Now, he reveals what happens when someone receives his grace. He says that he destroys the darkness in their heart with the lamp of wisdom.

Ignorance is often symbolized as darkness, but what is this lamp of wisdom that God talks about? At present, our senses, mind, and intellect are all material, while God is divine. Hence, we are unable to see him, hear him, know him, or be united with him. When God bestows his grace, he confers his divine *Yogmaya* energy upon the soul. It is also called *śhuddha* sattva (divine mode of goodness), which is distinct from the sattva guṇa (mode of goodness) of Maya. When we receive that *śhuddha* sattva energy, our senses, mind, and intellect become divine. To put it simply, by his grace, God bestows his divine senses, divine mind, and divine intellect to the soul. Equipped with these divine instruments, the soul is able to see God, hear God, know God, and be united with God. Hence, the Vedānt Darśhan states: *viśheṣhānugrahaśh cha* (3.4.38). "Only by God's grace does one gain divine knowledge." In this way, the torchlight that Shree Krishna refers to is his divine power. By the light of God's divine power, the darkness of the material energy is dispelled.

24. *The thought 'Who am I? ', will destroy all other thoughts, and like the stick used for stirring the burning pyre, it will itself in the end get destroyed. Then, there will arise Self-realization."*

NNK: This teaching on self-enquiry is by Ramana Maharshi. Thought is a discrete packet of consciousness-energy that is outward-turned. All other thoughts arise after the 'I' thought arises. The difference between other thoughts and the 'I' thought is that the 'I' thought is aware of its own existence. But, in its outward-turned nature, having identified with a mind and body, the 'I' thought limits this awareness of existence or existence-consciousness to 'I am the body'.

It is this ignorance that is the root of consciousness feeling trapped in a changing mind and world. It is the outward-turned nature of thought, that blocks knowledge of the Self of all. The quest 'Who am I?', turns this energy inward. The thought 'Who am I?', will destroy this outward nature of thought. All thoughts drop away in holding the quest. Finally, the thought 'Who am I?', too loses its need to be outside turned. Self-attention is natural. Self Realisation. The Self, which is natural self-attention, is the fire that is always burning. Hence, the quest 'Who am I?', is like stirring the burning pyre. The thought 'Who am I?', is like the stick used to burn all other thoughts. This thought too gets burnt in the self-attentive, self-luminous Self.

Dr. MK: What is self-realisation? How can we achieve this? To understand "Self Realisation", Lord Krishna gave the example of the Banyan tree as it has a large number of branches, leaves, and deep roots. To understand "Realisation", one has to consider it in inverted shape i.e. roots towards the top and branches below.

It has to be understood that there are large numbers of branches and leaves in the Banyan tree and the stem is not easily visible from the bottom due to its being inverted. Further, the roots are on top, and hence reaching the roots of such a tree is further difficult for self-realisation.

Further, such a tree is imperishable hence "Self Realisation" is ever-lasting. The branches are like ultimate knowledge and imperishable. Banyan tree has many branches, leaves, and roots, hence, to reach on top as such, one has to search the correct path. On following the correct path, one can reach self realisation stage. The branches of the tree are in all directions and developed from the sprout of the tree. Their development depends upon the development of the sprout and the size and shape of the tree would depend upon the sprout indirectly depending upon the environment and nourishment of the sprout.

Similarly, wisdom also depends upon the inherent attributes at birth and develops through knowledge. The knowledge develops from the senses due to three modes of material nature i.e., goodness, passion, and ignorance. Thus, senses control the knowledge.

With the attachment to the material world, the inverted form of the tree cannot be perceived, even not its beginning, and origin. To attain this knowledge, one needs a weapon of "Detachment". To understand and practise "Detachment", one has to reach the non-returnable stage of attachment. Such a condition is possible only when one takes asylum to the Supreme Power, and continuously follows the perpetual process of gaining wisdom.

To gain the wisdom of "Realisation", one has to renounce the ego and illusion in a way that it will never be adopted again i.e., to devoid them completely from the mind. Remember, illusion in the material world attracts one to attachments and desires.

25. ***Whenever and wherever the restless and unsteady mind wanders, one should bring it back and continually focus it on the Self."***

NNK: This teaching on the practice of self-enquiry is from the Bhagavad Gita. The practice is long and arduous. The mind is extremely difficult to understand and quieten. The outward-turned nature of thought takes the mind to other objects and thoughts.

It is said that, on an average, a human being has over 50,000 thoughts in a day. More than sixty percent of these are repetitive and wasteful. All thoughts make the 'I' thought feel dependent on forms and objects. So, the Gita asks the one interested in self-enquiry to be attentive whenever the mind rises as thought and runs after other thoughts or sense objects. One has to carefully withdraw one's attention from that thought and fix it in the self. With repeated, relentless practice, the other thoughts lose their power and the 'I' thought becomes one with its source, the Self.

Dr. MK: The Gita in Chapter 6 verse 26 says..

yato yato nishcharati manash chanchalam asthiram
tatas tato niyamyaitad atmanyeva vasham nayet

Whenever and wherever the restless and unsteady mind wanders, one should bring it back and continually focus it on God.

Success in meditation is not achieved in a day; the path to perfection is long and arduous. When we sit for meditation with the resolve to focus our mind upon God, we will find that ever so often, it wanders off in worldly ***saṅkalp and vikalp***. It is thus important to understand the three steps involved in the process of meditation:

With the intellect's power of discrimination, we decide that the world is not our goal. Hence, we forcefully remove the mind from the world. This requires effort.

Again, with the power of discrimination, we understand that God alone is ours, and God-realisation is our goal. Hence, we bring the mind to focus on God. This also requires effort. The mind comes away from God, and wanders back into the world. This does not require effort, it happens automatically.

When the third step happens by itself, ***sādhaks*** often become disappointed, "I tried so hard to focus upon God, but the mind went back into the world." Shri Krishna asks us not to feel disappointed. He says the mind is fickle and we should be prepared that it will wander off in the direction of its infatuation, despite our best efforts to control it. However, when it does wander off, we should once again repeat steps 1 and 2—take the mind away from the world and bring it back to God. Once again, we will experience that step 3 takes place by itself. We should not lose heart, and again repeat steps 1 and 2.

We will have to do this repeatedly. Then slowly, the mind's attachment to God will start increasing. And simultaneously, its detachment from the world will also increase. As this happens, it will become easier and easier to meditate. But in the beginning, we must be prepared for the battle involved in disciplining the mind.